# IMPROVING YOUR
# SELF IMAGE

Norman Wright

HARVEST HOUSE PUBLISHERS
Eugene, Oregon 97402

Except where otherwise indicated, all Scripture quotations in this book are taken from the New American Standard Bible, copyright © The Lockman Foundation 1960, 1962, 1963, 1968, 1971, 1972, 1973, 1975, 1977. Used by permission.

**IMPROVING YOUR SELF-IMAGE**

# CONTENTS

# Chapter One

# My Self-Image

What do you think when you look in a mirror? How do you feel about the person you see? Are you satisfied with yourself? If you are, you have a healthy self-image.

We all have an opinion of ourselves, whether we spend a lot of time thinking about it or not. Our self-image is the "map" that we consult about ourself. It is the mental picture of our self-identity. It is the "I am" feeling of a person. We either feel good about or we dislike or even hate and despise ourselves.

Where did our self-image come from, and how did it develop? The image we have of our *self* is built upon clusters of many memories. Very early in life we begin to form concepts and attitudes about ourselves, other people, and the world. Our self-concept is actually a cluster of attitudes about ourself—some favorable and some unfavorabe. Our mind never forgets an experience. We may not be conscious of it; but it is still there.

To use a simple illustration, you and I enter life carrying two containers—one in the left hand and one in the right. There is a plus sign on one container, and it collects all the positive information we receive about ourself. There is a minus sign on the other container, and here we gather all the negatives. These include sarcastic remarks, put-downs, looks of rejection, snubs, cruel statements, et cetera.

If we gather more positive than negative, we travel through life able to be productive and to experience joy and satisfaction. If we gather more in the negative container than in the positive, we move through life off-balance. Our self-image and personal sense of worth can become distorted, and we struggle against the load.

You have memories of situations in which you felt valuable and important. You have other memories which are not so pleasant. You might have experienced the pain of being rejected in front of a class at school or of a parent scolding you in front of your friends. You may have spent many hours building something, only to have it not work or have other people criticize it. You may have walked into a new school and no one talked to you for several days. Memories, both good and bad, form our self-image or our self-concept.

Years ago I went to an old-fashioned fun house. One of the experiences there centered around the hall of mirrors. For many of us this was a hilarious experience. There were mirrors which made us look fat, squat, as thin as a thermometer, cracked, fat with a small head, or thin with a big head. Mirrors, mirrors, mirrors with countless distorted reflections. Finally, at the end of the hall was a normal mirror which gave us back our normal look.

Some people pass through life never discerning their normal mirror. They live with constant self-distortions. These distortions filter out messages and comments which would bring their own evaluation into a proper perspective. Some of our mirrors distort us by reducing our value, while others distort us by overexpanding our value.

The Scriptures reflect us as we really are. But too often we forget or neglect this reflection. Most of us need the constant reminder of who and what we really are. It is not our evaluation of ourselves that counts, nor that of our friends or parents, but God's evaluation which brings clarity to the mirror.

What is it that reflects you adversely?

# Sources of Self-Esteem

## Parents

Self-esteem has to originate somewhere. Where did yours begin? Are you aware of the roots, the beginnings? For most of us, an important source is the relationship we had with our parents. The experience of being loved by our parents is the most important source of our self-esteem. People who do not experience love and acceptance from their parents seem to have difficulty in their love-response to other people. They also have difficulty in committing themselves to other people because they have never experienced their parents' commitment to them. People like this often move through life searching for love and commitment. Their intense need seems to be like a bottomless pit. Such people can never receive enough love and commitment. Or they may live in fear of losing what they have received and behave in such a manner that they push other people away. Still others who lack parental love refuse to take the risk involved in establishing the relationships which could give them love and commitment.

## Where Are You?

On a scale of 1-10 indicate your perception of your mother's love for you.

| 1 | 2 | 3 | 4 | 5 | 6 | 7 | 8 | 9 | 10 |
|---|---|---|---|---|---|---|---|---|---|
| not loved | | | | loved | | | very much loved | | |

On a scale of 1-10 indicate your perception of your father's love for you.

| 1 | 2 | 3 | 4 | 5 | 6 | 7 | 8 | 9 | 10 |
|---|---|---|---|---|---|---|---|---|----|
| not loved | | | | loved | | | | very much loved | |

Describe specifically what they did that convinced you that you were loved._____
_____
_____
_____

Describe specifically what they did that convinced you that they were committed to you.
_____
_____
_____

Describe the effect of your parents' response upon your sense of self esteem._____
_____
_____
_____

## Standards

The standards we set for ourselves are another source of our self-esteem. To what extent do your standards affect your self-esteem? Just what *are* your standards? Are they realistic? Are they yours or someone else's? Do they run your life or are you in charge of them?

I have heard many individuals make comments such as: "I feel good when I accomplish everything on my list," "I'm okay when I don't make any mistakes," "I feel good about myself when everyone likes me," or "I need to have every room in my house spotless." Most of us gain self-approval by living up to our standards. We feel good about ourselves and we feel competent. Living up to standards is not the problem; the difficulty occurs when the standards are so extreme and out of balance that their attainment is rare. This creates guilt, depression, and a lowered sense of worth. Standards need to be evaluated objectively in the following manner.

1. Are they really what *I* want for my life?
2. When did they originate?
3. Am I able to feel okay about myself even when they are not met? Can I accept my humanity?
4. Have I asked other competent and objective people to help me evaluate them?
5. Are they standards which Scripture suggests?

Now list five of the standards you have for your life. Describe how these relate to your self-esteem.

1. _____

2. _____

3. _____

4. _____

5. _____

_____

_____

_____

_____

_____

*Chapter Two*

# The Effect
# of Rejection

Most people have experienced some degree of rejection. Many have experienced *intense* rejection. Infants and children especially need positive experiences to enhance their emotional growth and emotional health, both of which are so essential to their development. Isolation, rejection, and deprivation seriously affect the life of a child. The Word of God cautions against damaging a child's self-concept: "Fathers, do not provoke or irritate or fret your children—do not be hard on them or harass them; lest they become discouraged and sullen and morose and feel inferior and frustrated; do not break their spirit'' (Colossians 3:21 AMP). (For more information on building the self-concept of a child, read *Hide or Seek,* by Dr. James Dobson, and *Your Child's Self-Esteem,* by Dorothy Briggs.)

Eartha Kitt, the well-known singer and entertainer, tells in her autobiography, *Thursday's Child,* how as a young child she experienced intense rejection. She felt rejected by her own father, who had deserted her mother. When her mother had the opportunity to remarry, it was with the condition that Eartha be given up. She was turned over to a relative who did not want her either, and she lived in loneliness, with scorn and abuse directed toward her.

She finally discovered that she could win some acceptance and approval from this relative by singing in church. So she began to sing and perform as a means of gaining acceptance and approval. But for many years, even after she had become a famous star, the rejection she had experienced in her childhood continued to make her unhappy and miserable. She was an easy mark for her exploitive ''friends'' because she still desperately needed acceptance and approval. Only after many years was she able to accept herself as worthwhile.

Eartha Kitt struggled with put-downs like you and I do. They hurt.

Do you know what a put-down is? It's a statement designed to demoralize, downgrade, and devastate a person. People sling them at us and we put ourselves down as well. Have you experienced some like these?

"You won't grow up to amount to any good."

"You're nothing but family trash."

"You're not acceptable and never will be."

"You are not important."

"You don't measure up."

Perhaps you make statements like these to yourself. Perhaps your parents made them, or your friends.

Sometimes the put-downs are directed at where you live, what you own, how you dress, how you wear your hair, et cetera.

If you are struggling with your self-image, look for your list of put-downs. You may be believing what other people have said to you. Why not challenge them? What would happen if you did?

The Bible is full of verses that describe the view that God has of us. Does He ever put us down? *Never!* Actually, He has a very high view of us, His creation. Look at these verses, for example:

Ephesians 1:6      "To the praise of the glory of His grace, which He fully bestowed on us in the Beloved."

1 Corinthians 4:7      "For who regards you as superior? And what do you have that you did not

receive? But if you did receive it, why do you boast as if you had not received it?''

Genesis 1:27

''And God created man in His own image; in the image of God He created him; male and female He created them.''

Psalm 8:5

''Yet Thou hast made him a little lower than God, and dost crown him with glory and majesty!''

Jeremiah 29:11

'' 'For I know the plans that I have for you,' declares the Lord, 'plans for welfare and not for calamity, to give you a future and a hope.' ''

Psalm 139:17,18

''How precious also are Thy thoughts to me, O God! How vast is the sum of them! If I should count them, they would outnumber the sand. When I awake, I am still with Thee.''

1 John 3:1

''See how great a love the Father has bestowed upon us, that we should be called children of God; and such we are. For this reason the world does not know us, because it did not know Him.''

Ephesians 1:18 ''I pray that the eyes of your heart may be enlightened, so that you may know what is the hope of His calling, what are the riches of the glory of His inheritance in the saints.''

Jude 24 ''Now to Him who is able to keep you from stumbling, and to make you stand in the presence of His glory blameless with great joy.''

Adults experience rejection just as much as children do. It may take a different form, however. There are many forms of rejection. Regardless of what kind, the result is the same—pain. Rejection can be direct, such as someone telling you they don't care for you or they no longer love you. It can be indirect, such as when our children reject the value system or beliefs that we have attempted to teach them. A child or adolescent may choose to behave in a way that is totally opposite to the way his parents behave. Some parents believe that if their moral code is rejected, they themselves are being rejected also. They believe that *who they are* is expressed by *what they believe* about right and wrong behavior.

In his book *The Wounded Parent,* Dr. Guy Greenfield says:

> Morality represents a cluster of beliefs, values, ideals, and convictions about what is important in life. The moral standards I live by reflect my personal perception of life. I see life through the lenses of certain values. Since I have tried to pass these values on to my children, what they do with my values is what they do with me.... A rejection of the moral codes of one's parents will likely be taken personally by the parents. We parents are too wrapped up in our moral convictions to separate ourselves intellectually from those convictions and not feel the emotional pain of rejection when our children disappoint us with their behavior.[1]

When children reject a parent's lifestyle, the parent feels rejected. This can include economic level, standard of living, cultural tastes, et cetera. A child's rejection may not be an angry, defiant act but simply, "I'd rather work three days a week and bum around the other four," or "I'd rather live in a log cabin and drive a jeep. That's the great lifestyle." An alternate choice of lifestyle is taken both as a rejection and as an act of ingratitude. But is it really?

An even more personal rejection and hurt

occurs when children turn their backs on our faith and our church. For many parents, this is embarrassing and is interpreted as a sign of parental failure. One of the deepest hurts occurs when parental love, whether conditional or unconditional, is rejected. It is difficult to understand why a flesh-and-blood child would reject a parent's love. After all, doesn't every person want love, and especially the love of a parent?

The longer we allow the sense of rejection to linger, the more erosion occurs of our self-esteem. None of us like to be rejected, and as parents we will experience disappointment with our children. In fact, the greater the expectations that we have for our children the more we see them as our major source of happiness, the greater the potential for being let down.

Our sense of self-esteem and our happiness in life is not solely dependent upon how our children turn out or respond. If it is, we have an overinvestment in them.

Our self-image is not built upon people outside ourselves. Yes, we will feel hurt through rejection and disappointment, but this can be a time for growth and strengthening our life. Security and self-esteem come from *within,* not from without, through a personal relationship with God.

Dr. Greenfield's advice to a parent who has been wounded by a child is this: "As you, a wounded parent, attempt to build a new relationship with your rebellious child, it is also important for you not to neglect yourself. The self-image of a wounded parent is not likely to be in good shape. It probably bears the trappings of failure and defeat. A battered self-image needs to be repaired. Yours may even need a transplant!

"Some people who have undergone plastic surgery suddenly developed what seemed to be a new self-image. Believing in their new attractiveness and beauty, they began accepting and even loving themselves in a healthy way. You may not need plastic surgery in order to develop a new self-image. God has His own unique methods of the spirit."[2]

Our thought life and the value judgments we make about ourself can intensify our feelings of rejection and lessen self-esteem. If my child chooses an alternate direction I may think, "Something is wrong with me. Something is wrong with our home life, our Christian life."

There are two facts to remember. First, we as parents *will* make mistakes because we are imperfect. Second, you could do the best job possible and your child could still choose to accept a different lifestyle.

Failure causes us to forget who we really are and what we have been given. You see, as believers a new image has been given to us.

1 Corinthians 15:49　"And just as we have borne the image of the earthy, we shall bear the image of the heavenly."

We are in a constant state of being changed.

2 Corinthians 3:18 "But we all, with unveiled face beholding as in a mirror the glory of the Lord, are being transformed into the same image from glory to glory, just as from the Lord, the Spirit."

Galatians 4:19 "My children, with whom I am again in labor until Christ is formed in you."

We may think we have failed. Perhaps we have and perhaps we haven't. In any case, God is still changing us. Building a solid and new self-image means recognizing the new image of God in Christ which God is creating in us. When we understand this truth, the behavior and beliefs of other people will not cause our self-esteem to crumble.

*Stop for a moment and answer these questions.*

How do you treat yourself? _____

_____

_____

_____

Have you ever thought of yourself as being a parent to yourself? _____

_____

_____

_____

What kind of parent are you?_____
_____
_____
_____

Do you treat yourself with scorn and disrespect?
_____
_____
_____

Do you punish yourself? _____
_____
_____
_____

Do you expect and demand too much of yourself? _____
_____
_____
_____

What is your God like? _____
_____
_____
_____

How do you know? _____
_____
_____
_____
_____

"For through the grace given to me I say to every man among you not to think more highly of himself than he ought to think but to think so as to have sound judgment, as God has allotted to each a measure of faith" (Romans 12:3). Our thoughts about ourselves should be based upon "sober judgment." How else could sober judgment be phrased? Perhaps "sound-minded" or even "sane." Our self-evaluation is to be a sane evaluation.

Our view of God affects our self-image and our ability to love others as well. Some people view through the eyes of their culture. For others their false idea of God comes from their parents. If parental love is conditional, we tend to believe God's love is the same. A child quickly learns that he is loved more when he is quiet, eats all his food, keeps his room neat, and brings home "Bs" and "As" on his report card. Because of learning to expect love for what we do and not for what we are, we begin to believe that we have to earn or merit God's love. Unfortunately, our internal beliefs about God do not mature as we grow older, and they are stuck at an infantile level.

By having a misperception of who God is, we limit our capacity for developing fully our self-image.

God created us in His own image and likeness. But have we tended to create God in our own image and likeness or our parents' image and likeness? If I am judgmental of myself, do I see God as a judge?

God is not a policeman, unfair judge, or spiteful tyrant—God is fair, just, loving, holy, righteous, faithful, and good. (If you would like to build an accurate perception of God, read *Your God Is Too Small*, by J.B. Phillips, and *Knowing God*, by J.I. Packer.)

How does God see us and what does He want for us? Dr. James Packer described the answer in this way:

> There is tremendous relief in knowing that His love to me is utterly realistic, based at every point on prior knowledge of the worst about me, so that no discovery now can disillusion Him about me, in the way I am so often disillusioned about myself, and quench His determination to bless me. There is, certainly, great cause for humility in the thought that He sees all the twisted things about me that my fellow-men do not see...and that He sees more corruption in me than that which I see in myself.... He wants me as His friend, and desires to be my friend, and has given His Son to die for me in order to realise this purpose.[3]

Past rejections may continue to haunt a person's self-concept and reinforce it. But the influence of the past can be broken.

Dr. Maxwell Maltz illustrates this in a story about a very brave man who insisted on fighting oppressive forces to forget a horrible past and find a worthwhile present.

His past:

"They lined us up against a wall—over 100 of us—and then they mowed us down with machine guns."

This man wanted me to operate on him. I looked at him—he was in his late forties, short, blue eyes, graying blonde hair—and wondered how he had survived that concentration camp in Germany in 1944.

"I was wounded in the face here—in the jaw and neck. My friends who rescued me put a piece of rug against the bleeding wound; they hid me in the concentration camp. The rest were all dead and buried en masse in a deep, wide hole in the ground." He paused as if to see again in his mind those horrible events.

"The months passed. I had fever and I thought I would die. Many days I can't remember what happened. All I know is that somehow I survived. And then the American soldiers came."

He looked at the floor. Then, after a deep breath, "My mother, father, sister, brothers—all gone. I traveled all over the world. But I could not forget."

He wiped his eyes, and his wife (whom he had married a year earlier) put her arm around him. "Do you think you could help, doctor?" she asked.

"Maybe. Why did you wait so long? It is 25 years since it happened."

"I wasn't ready."

"I don't understand."

"You see, I wanted to remember. I didn't want to forget. It was comforting to remember the past—before those terrible times—when things were all right and we were happy."

"And you're ready now?"

"Yes, I am."

I studied his face. A deep, indented scar on the right side under his chin distorted it terribly—it was as if he were two people, one handsome, the other distorted.

"I want to forget," he said. "I want a new start, a new life."

I told him I would operate and that I would also remove the tatoo numbers on his arm.

It was a rather difficult operation, but when I finished the results were splendid. His face was symmetrical again.

I had operated under local anesthesia. "Finished," I said.

Then he made a request. "Can I take a look?"

In approximately 45 years of plastic surgery, having performed something like 20,000 operations, I have never heard such a request at such a moment.

I took my gloves off and handed him a mirror. He studied himself at length, then whispered, "Thanks, doctor, thanks."

A week later the final stitches were removed, and the stitches on his arm. He looked at his face. He beamed with satisfaction. All he said was "Thanks," but the look on his face told me that, in spite of all the agonies of his past, he had wiped them from his imagination and was living in the present. Freed from the past, he was a new person—a person he once had been.

He gave me a present before he left. It was a rag doll. That is his business. He manufactures dolls and ships them all over North and South America.

That night I thought about this brave man who refused to allow his imagination to remain a wasteland of negation, who insisted on escaping from his nightmarish memories and on using the power of his imagination for creative living in the present.[4]

*Chapter Three*

# The Cycle of Negative Thinking

Once a particular attitude toward oneself has been formed, it usually influences one's future judgments and becomes fairly strongly set.

A child who gets the notion that he is incapable, either as a result of failure or of being called incompetent by other people, will respond to future experiences according to this belief.

Every new negative judgment tends to reinforce the negative belief or negative self-image. The result is that a vicious cycle is set in motion. Each new negative judgment reinforces the already-present negative self-image.

This in turn reinforces a negative interpreta

tion of future experiences, which further solidifies the negative self-concept.

The image you have of yourself is determined mostly through your interpersonal relationships. Your self-image is the result of the interpretation you make of your own involvements with other people. Your interpretation is not what others actually think, but what *you think* others think of you!

It is this subjective interpretation that is important to your self-image. This interpretation feeds it positively or negatively.

Many people experience negative thoughts and feelings about themselves from time to time. But a negative self-image is always associated with negative value judgments. Not all people who regard themselves as physically, mentally, or socially lacking in certain areas consider these to be problems, nor are they repelled by them. They either accept their limitations or try to change them.

Some people, however, make negative value judgments regarding their deficiencies. They tell themselves:

"I must be bad or worthless."
"Only bad people have these traits."
"It's my fault that I have them."
"I'll always be this way."
"There's no hope of changing."

The attitudes that make up our self-image continually reinforce themselves, as illustrated on the next page.

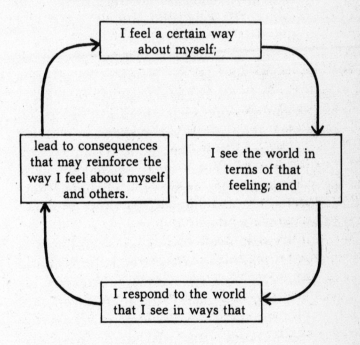

Self-image has a controlling influence on the mind. A person's opinion of himself affects his interpretation of life. A person who thinks unrealistically about himself does so because his self-concept is malformed. If it is severely malformed, he will reject even positive information and responses about himself which other people seek to give him.

The individual who has a good self-image feels worthwhile. He feels good about himself and likes himself. He accepts both his positive qualities and his weaknesses. He is confident but he is also realistic. He can handle other people's reactions, both positive and negative. He sets out to accomplish what he is capable of doing and feels that other people will respond to him. He has confidence in his perceptions, ability, and judgments. He is not afraid to become involved in the lives of other people nor to allow others to become involved in his life. And he is not defensive.

But the person who has a poor self-image is just the opposite. He doesn't trust himself and is usually apprehensive about expressing his ideas for fear of attracting the attention of other people. He may withdraw and live in the shadow of others or his social group. He is overly aware of himself and often has a morbid preoccupation with his problems.

Because he is so preoccupied with himself, he does not correctly perceive the attitudes that other people have toward him. He believes that other people must feel the same about him as he feels about himself. Since he feels that other people do not want to include him in their group, he is hesitant to join them for fear of rejection. He can mingle with people but is hesitant to become honestly and openly involved with them. His avoidance of others has the effect of reinforcing his low self-image.

## Self-Depreciation

Self-depreciation may be the result of direct self-criticism, projection of our attitudes onto others, or comparison of ourself with others. It may range in degree from slight to intense, and may range in frequency from a passing thought to a total preoccupation.

### *Direct Self-Criticism*

This is the most common type of self-depreciation. Statements such as:

"I'm so stupid"

"I'm so clumsy"

"I'm so inconsiderate" and

"There I go again—I can't even keep the house clean for five minutes"

are typical of a person who engages in constant, direct self-criticism. The most common words used in self-criticism are dumb, stupid, bad, inadequate, silly, lazy, and unworthy. We often use these words without thinking, even though they have no value and do not even belong in our vocabulary.

We can all find things for which to criticize ourselves, but self-criticism keeps us from growing and makes us miserable.

## Projection of Self Onto Others

Sometimes it seems that our self-depreciation comes from other people instead of from ourselves. We say:

> "They sure think I'm dumb,"
> "They don't like me," or
> "I bet they laugh at my efforts."

We project onto others the attitudes that we have about ourself. Not only do we attribute untrue attitudes to others, but we also behave toward them as though they actually held these attitudes.

## Comparison of Self with Others

When we compare ourselves with others we usually come out second best. You might say to yourself about a close friend, "I'm really not as good as he is because he is so kind, beautiful, intelligent, sensitive, handy, helpful, popular, insightful, and clever." You may even say that you are deeply in love with another person but add, "But I'm no good for him (or her)."

We all compare ourselves with other people at one time or another. We can do it in both a joking manner and a serious vein. The older I get the less hair I seem to have on my forehead. In fact, it looks like a great ski slope. As I see myself in different poses in pictures, I'm often taken aback by how little hair is actually there! I have two colleagues who have an overabundance of hair. I notice this as they make comments about the blinding shine on my forehead, and I make comments to them about their shaggy mops! We enjoy bantering back and forth. And this is a degree of comparison.

Comparison is a very poor source of self-esteem. By comparing ourselves with other people we end up feeling either good or, more likely, bad about ourselves, depending upon our subjective evaluation. If we see another person as more eloquent, more gifted, having a better build, more attractive, wealthier, a better friend, more at ease in social situations, or having more opportunities, we will probably feel down. But if the situation is reversed, we will probably feel better about ourselves.

Comparison can eventually become a motivating force in our life to get ahead, to be better than others, to be first, et cetera.

For over 17 years I have taught at a graduate-level seminary. Each year I encounter students who are so motivated by grades that their entire focus and perspective on life is dominated by this pursuit. Some of them are not satisfied by obtaining an "A." They want the highest "A" in the class or on an exam!

When we try to use comparison as a means of feeling good about ourselves, it is difficult to be content, satisfied, or stable in our feelings about ourselves. There will always be other

people who are more competent, better
qualified, richer, better-looking, smarter, or
quicker than we are. Comparison indicates that
we are status-conscious.

Dr. Norman Vincent Peale tells the story of
a young wife who came to consult him:

> She was upset and frightened. Her
> husband was under consideration for
> a promotion, an important one. But it
> was the custom of that particular com-
> pany to have a party at which top exec-
> utives had a chance to observe the
> employee under social conditions.
> Wives were always asked to this affair,
> because the company believed, quite
> rightly, that a man and his wife are an
> inseparable team—when you deal with
> one you are dealing with the other.
>
> I said to this young woman, "Why
> are you so concerned? You are able to
> handle yourself."
>
> "Oh, Dr. Peale," she said, and her
> eyes were actually full of tears, "all
> those other wives have been to colleges
> like Smith or Vassar or Wellesley. I
> never got past high school. They'll talk
> about things I'm not familiar with. I
> just know I'll be so tense I'll say or do
> something dumb and ruin Jim's
> chances for this promotion. I can't
> bring myself to go, and yet I can't
> refuse to go. Oh, what shall I do?"

Timidity, you see, timidity even in the presence of a routine situation.

I said to her, "Look, you're a very pretty girl, you dress well; you have honesty and your own quiet charm. Don't worry about these wives from Wellesley. They don't know all that much, anyway. Just be yourself. The trouble with a lot of people is that they always try to copy somebody else. If the Creator wanted us all to be alike, He would have made us that way. You are the only person in the world like you. Think of that: millions of people and only one like you! You are unique and very special. So you just walk into that party and be yourself, your own attractive self. Mix right in with those people and you will shake off this inferiority complex. Go among them and say to yourself, 'I can do all things through Christ who strengthens me.' Just imagine yourself as charming, natural, and likeable and you will come off okay."[1]

When we compare ourselves to other people we usually fail to thank and praise God for the giftedness, potential, and ability of both others and ourselves! By accepting our own abilities as well as those of others, we can work together as a complete team.

What we say about the qualities of others and

ourselves makes a big difference. We may say, "That other person has so many abilities and opportunities," or "He can do that job in half the time I can," or "Look at their home and furniture. It's unbelievable!"

But we also need to say, "Isn't that great!" or "That's wonderful!" or "I'm really glad for them." It may take us some time to work through our perceived lacks, hurts, and attitudes. But in God's eyes our status has already been given to us.

If you feel inadequate, sometimes it is a good idea to ask yourself, "Inadequate compared to what!" I've known people who were despondent and downcast because they allowed themselves to become victims of too-great expectations. A young man about to enter college sought me out to talk about his inferiority feelings. It didn't take much perception to see that the trouble lay in his relationship with his father, or rather, with his father's memory, since the parent had died some years before. That father had been a great athlete, an all-American fullback, in fact, and foolishly the boy's mother was forever reminding him of this. The boy himself simply didn't have the physique to be a football player, or an outstanding athlete of any kind. But instead of accepting this fact, he was letting it make him miserable.

"Look," I said to him after I had asked a few questions. "You're a good student—probably better than your father was. You're a fine chess player. You've been the editor of your high school yearbook. You're just using the wrong yardstick, that's all! Be proud of your father, sure. But also be proud of yourself, because you deserve to be!"

Nine times out of ten, as was the case with this youngster, a feeling of inferiority is nothing but a state of mind. It was Milton who wrote:

> The mind is its own place,
> and in itself can make a heav'n of hell,
> a hell of heav'n.[2]

Who have you compared yourself to in the past five years?_____

_____

_____

_____

How did you feel or think or behave because of the comparison?_____

_____

_____

_____

What can you do the next time you begin to compare yourself with other people?_____

_____

_____

_____

There is nothing wrong with introspection that leads to a correct evaluation of ourself. In fact Scripture encourages us to search our own hearts. But it does not encourage us to compare ourselves unfavorably with other people.

And now a word about failure—as sure a thing as death and taxes. What if I fail in some area of my life? What if I really blow it? How can I ever regain my self-esteem, especially if what I have done will be with me the rest of my life?

Listen to the words of Dale Galloway:

> On a cloudy day in the fall of 1969, I was sitting in a restaurant on Southeast 82nd Street in Portland, Oregon, unaware of the catastrophe about to strike my life. Seated across the table from me was the girl I had fallen in love with as a freshman in college. We had married in the summer of 1957 and had struggled together to get me through college, seminary, and the beginning years of my pastoral ministry. Now the struggle for economic survival was over. At age 30, I was enjoying the success of pastoring one of the larger churches of our

denomination in the State of Oregon. The future had never looked brighter.

Then it happened. The volcano of pent-up emotions erupted. My wife of twelve years angrily pointed her finger at me and said, "I do not love you. I never have loved you, and I'm going to divorce you." The sentence of death had been pronounced.

Nothing worse could have happened to me as a minister brought up in a God-fearing, Bible-believing, conservative church and home. The collapse of my marriage meant that in the eyes of my church family I was a failure. A failure as a husband, a failure as a minister, and even a failure as a Christian. At this time I experienced the emptiness of feeling rejected, unloved. Is there any more devastating feeling?

Dale described just how devastating this experience and its aftermath were in his first book, *Dream a New Dream*.

Having lost all sense of time, I wandered aimlessly along an unknown beach in the State of Washington. I was sobbing uncontrollably every step of the way. As the sun was going down and darkness was closing in, I dropped down on the beach completely exhausted. For me the sun had stopped shining; there was only darkness.

"Where the hell are you, God?" I shouted. Just a few brief months before, I would not have believed any true minister of God would think such words, let alone shout them angrily again and again at the top of his voice.... Before ending up on that beach, at the bottom emotionally, I had gone four days without food, fasting and praying, calling on God to, by some miracle, save our marriage. Now, as I lay on the beach, I knew the marriage was over. My life as a minister would soon be wrecked. My children would be taken many miles away from me. Never before had we had a divorce in my immediate family, and I didn't see how any of the family could ever accept me again.

My father, whom I loved and for whom I had great respect, had not only been a minister for as long as I could remember, but had for the past thirty years been the head administrator of our denomination in the State of Ohio. My dad's brother had also been a prominent minister. Both my grandfathers had helped to pioneer, and had literally sacrificed everything they had, to help establish the denomination that our family now enjoyed so very much. I grew up knowing how the church thought almost as well as I knew my own thoughts.

Instinctively, I knew that there was no way that the people from this conservative, evangelical background would ever be able to understand my divorce. I would forever be, in their eyes, a "second-class citizen."

In my brokenness and out of the anguish of my soul I cried, "Where the hell are you, God? Don't you care? Haven't I served you since I was fifteen years old? Haven't I tried to do everything that you have wanted me to do? I have never said 'no' to anything you wanted in my life. Where are you now? Don't you even care that I'm going down for the last time?"[3]

The good news is that Dale Galloway did not stay at this place in his life. Today he is ministering to other people in similar circumstances. He is also pastoring a large congregation in Portland, Oregon. But how did he move ahead? What made the difference? Dale said:

For the first time my will to die was stronger than my will to live because everything that I lived for I was losing.

Do you know what saved my life? Do you know what kept me going when I didn't feel like getting out of bed in the morning? What gave me hope when people around me said I was a wash-out? I got into the heart of the

Bible and encountered Jesus in a new, fresh way.

I saw Him suffer and die on the cross for my sins. He died for my failings, my shortcomings, my mistakes, my sins, and whatever else anybody wants to call it. The truth is that whatever is wrong with me and whatever is wrong with you, He died on that cross to forgive it and make it right.[4]

The question is not "Can I start over again?" The question is "Do I want to change?"

*What a person thinks of himself largely determines the kind of life he will live.* If a person sees himself as inferior to other people (regardless of talents and abilities), he will probably do inferior work. Conversely, individuals with lesser ability but with higher self-esteem have been known to work above the level of their capabilities. Psychological studies seem to confirm the hypothesis that people with low self-esteem tend to be less creative and more anxious, and are less likely to have successful experiences than persons with high self-esteem.

An Iowa schoolteacher decided to demonstrate the black-white racial problem by dividing her third-grade pupils into blue-eyed and brown-eyed children. On a certain day the brown-eyed children were placed in the back of the room. The blue-eyed children seated in front of the room were told, "Brown-eyed children can't read as well as you can, can't color as well as you can, and are not as bright as you are."

That day the brown-eyed children did not do as well as the others because they believed they were inferior, as they had been told. They performed according to the image of themselves that had been created by the teacher. Many people who in the past have been told they were inferior, or inferred inferiority from the attitudes of others, are today emotionally crippled.

In his book *Self-Worth*, Joseph Aldrich says:

> ...Calling an eagle a chicken does not make it a chicken, even if it lives in a chicken coop, crows on a fencepost, and pecks at table scraps in the barnyard! But what a tragedy for the eagle. By assuming a chicken identity, the king of birds forfeits the sky, the far horizons, and a wind-swept nest that crowns a mountain.
>
> Even more pathetic, however, is a person who would stoop to treat an eagle like a chicken. Jonathan Edwards understood this travesty when he wrote:
>
>> The ultimate good is to treat something according to its true value.
>
> Eagles must be treated like eagles. Not to treat an eagle like an eagle, then, would be the ultimate sin against eagledom.
>
> Eagles who perceive themselves as

chickens will think, act, and respond like chickens (and probably treat fellow eagles like barnyard fowl as well). People who perceive themselves to be donkeys will line up to be saddled. In large measure, you become what you think you are—even if your perceptions are distorted. If you think you have no value, then for all *practical* purposes...you're probably right.[5]

You and I tend to behave according to how we are treated. If a child in a home is treated like he is worthless, he feels like he's worthless, and so on. It's a never-ending, vicious circle.

*Chapter Four*

# Love Yourself

Walter Trobisch has graphically described the vicious cycle which develops in interpersonal relationships: "We are unable to love others because we have not learned to love ourselves. We cannot learn to love ourselves because we are not loved by others or are unable to accept their love. We are not loved by others because we are unable to love them or we love them only "out of duty." We are unable to love them because we have not learned to love ourselves. And thus it begins all over again."[1]

Joshua Liebman in *Peace of Mind* said: "He who hates himself, who does not have a proper regard for his own capacities...can have no respect for others; deep within himself he will hate his brothers when he sees in them his own marred image."[2]

In the list of causes for depression, a poor self-image is near the top. It is easy for a person to become depressed over his apparent life situation. The depression reinforces the low self-image. As the depression deepens, the low self-image is further reinforced.

People struggle desperately to either maintain a good self-image or obtain acceptance from others. The attempts at both often prove to be more destructive than constructive. Snell and Gail Putney described "the person who is caught up in the quest for indirect self-acceptance" as "more concerned with making a favorable impression on others than with seeing an honest reflection of himself. He attempts to manipulate the way he appears to others. Consequently, he cannot credit any favorable image they may reflect, for he has good reason to think that what he sees is only his most flattering angle.

"Moreover, he is likely to become preoccupied with the limitations he is struggling to conceal from others, with the result that these 'defects' loom disproportionately large in his self-image. The person who seeks indirect self-acceptance thus begins by trying to manipulate the image he presents to others and ends by having a distorted self-image, in which his defects are magnified."[3]

Hiding and deceiving become part of the game

of life. Arthur DeJong said about this type of behavior:

> To prove his worth to others and to himself, the person with low self-esteem often takes on the image of "worker" or "helper" or both. The worker goes at his work feverishly and with an eye to perfection. The helper feels worthwhile when he has helped someone and when that person responds affirmatively. Since he is never convinced of his worth, the person repeats this pattern endlessly. Indeed, it becomes a need, and therefore a personality trait.
>
> Because the person with low self-esteem wishes to be accepted by others, both to prove his worth and to gain interpersonal relationships, he is often guided more by what he thinks will please others than by his own desires, or by what he thinks is right. He is not his own man, but rather a victim of his feelings and need. Down deep he hates himself because of this lack of integrity. Thus he is caught in a vicious circle.[4]

Even the successful person who feels good about himself can be caught up with problems of self-image.

> A few years ago, a certain young man became nationally known for his box-

ing exploits. His picture was prominently displayed in numerous papers and magazines. He had appeared in international amateur events and achieved an outstanding record. Observers predicted great success for him in professional boxing. As predicted, the young man evolved into a first-class professional fighter. Developed carefully by a skillful manager, he won matches repeatedly. In a few short years, he emerged as the world champion of his weight division.

But now, problems began to appear. Because he had lived so long with the self-picture of a champion, he began to dread defeat. He had held his title several years when these fears came to dominate him. He knew age was slowing him somewhat and that he could never fully regain the abilities of more youthful days. Gradually his personality turned inward. He avoided his friends, the press and even most friendly conversational contacts. Hating to face the world, he employed disguise artists so that he could move freely in the streets without being noticed. He had no more worlds to conquer, and the empire he owned was threatened frequently by young aspirants. Finally he became sullen and sour, and his wife divorced him.

After refusing a number of challenges to his title, he realized that he must face the possibility of defeat or be dethroned by default. One day, an improbable young upstart challenged his title. Accepting this challenge seemed to the champion to be an easy way to maintain prestige, so the fight was on.

He prepared badly, and the fight showed it. He fought as though he were already defeated. His moves were halting and badly timed. In the second round, a crushing uppercut caught his chin, and he was counted out. The championship was gone, and a shaky self-image was finally completely shattered.

Very likely, the fear of loss defeated him long before his final match. From that time on, he turned in his loneliness and self-disrespect to dissipation and died a pauper. Even the way of death was a confirmation of his self-perception. Seeing himself as worthless, he acted accordingly and hastened his demise.

The boxer's story shows how desperately people struggle to fend off loss of image. The need for the image to be protected constitutes a fundamental mental health problem. Many business and professional organizations no longer fire the tired and spent executive. They appoint him a vice-president on a consulting basis. We say that he is kicked upstairs. This has become the humane way of dealing with loss of ability or prowess. It preserves the man's self-esteem and still allows his useful talents to be applied.

So we struggle to see ourselves in essentially positive ways. If distortion of self-image is necessary, we resort to it. We prize our self-perceptions and psychogical integrity more than our sanity.[5]

"Thou shalt love thy neighbor as thyself" means to consider the needs of other people as equally important with your own, to value other people's opinions equally with your own, to respect the rights of other people equally with your own rights. Other people are not less important than you, but they are also not *more* important than you. This type of thinking takes effort, especially if it is contrary to what we have been taught. Sometimes it is easier and more comfortable to degrade yourself and believe that others' opinions of you are more important than your own.

The Scriptures teach us an important truth about our self-worth. Your life, including your opinions, feelings, wants, and needs, is not less valuable or important, nor more valuable or important than anyone else's.

When Jesus said, "Greater love has no one than this, that one lay down his life for his friends" (John 15:13), He prepared the way for us to be able to love ourselves in the purest sense. Condemnation, guilt, despair, self-degradation, shame, and self-hate have all been nailed to the cross in His body. By His taking our sin on the cross with Him, we are set free to live healthy and abundant lives with wholesome, pure, swept-clean attitudes. When our lives are really beautiful in the eyes of God, they are pure and clean in the holiest sense.[6]

## A SELF-IMAGE CHECKLIST

How is your self-image? Answer these questions honestly. If you are unsure of some of the answers, ask a close friend to discuss your answers with you.

|  | | Most of the time | Some- times | Rarely |
|---|---|---|---|---|
| 1. | Can you handle a crisis situation? | | | |
| 2. | In coping with life's stresses, do you tend to blame other people, circumstances, or even God? | | | |
| 3. | Do you recognize your own opinion and worth? | | | |
| 4. | Is it difficult for you to accept other people? | | | |
| 5. | Do people frequently seem to contradict your opinion of yourself? | | | |

6. Do people tell you that you are better-looking than you feel you are? \_\_\_\_\_  \_\_\_\_\_  \_\_\_\_\_

7. Are you easily controlled or swayed by circumstances or what other people think and do? \_\_\_\_\_  \_\_\_\_\_  \_\_\_\_\_

8. Do you tend to follow the crowd? \_\_\_\_\_  \_\_\_\_\_  \_\_\_\_\_

9. Do you think that you are of little help to other people? \_\_\_\_\_  \_\_\_\_\_  \_\_\_\_\_

10. Are you often defensive? \_\_\_\_\_  \_\_\_\_\_  \_\_\_\_\_

11. Do you have bouts with depression? \_\_\_\_\_  \_\_\_\_\_  \_\_\_\_\_

12. Do you consistently perform poorly or not at all? \_\_\_\_\_  \_\_\_\_\_  \_\_\_\_\_

13. Do you accept your appearance as it is without fussing over it? \_\_\_\_\_  \_\_\_\_\_  \_\_\_\_\_

14. Do you watch for every defect in your performance in order to perfect it? \_\_\_\_\_  \_\_\_\_\_  \_\_\_\_\_

15. Do you behave in a manner that repels people? \_\_\_\_\_  \_\_\_\_\_  \_\_\_\_\_

16. Do you find it difficult to accept criticism? \_\_\_\_\_  \_\_\_\_\_  \_\_\_\_\_

17. Are you afraid of other people because you might fail? \_\_\_\_\_  \_\_\_\_\_  \_\_\_\_\_

Your answers to these questions may give you some indication of the level of your self-image.

*Chapter Five*

# The Depressive Triad

What occurs in the thought process of a person with a low self-image? There is similarity between the thinking pattern of this person and one who is experiencing significant depression. The model of thinking of a depressed person can be thought of as a triad of thought directions. This model is called the depressive triad as diagrammed on the following page.

The first thinking pattern in the depressive triad occurs in the mind of a person who *construes the world and his interactions with the world as an unpleasant and unfortunate ordeal in life.* His interpretation of events is characterized by

# DEPRESSIVE TRIAD

### *Thinking Patterns*

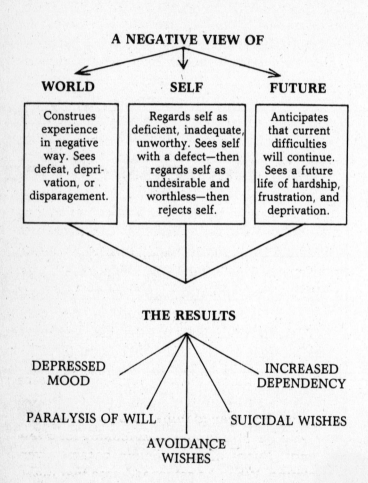

**A NEGATIVE VIEW OF**

**WORLD**     **SELF**     **FUTURE**

| | | |
|---|---|---|
| Construes experience in negative way. Sees defeat, deprivation, or disparagement. | Regards self as deficient, inadequate, unworthy. Sees self with a defect—then regards self as undesirable and worthless—then rejects self. | Anticipates that current difficulties will continue. Sees a future life of hardship, frustration, and deprivation. |

**THE RESULTS**

DEPRESSED
MOOD                    INCREASED
                        DEPENDENCY

PARALYSIS OF WILL        SUICIDAL WISHES

AVOIDANCE
WISHES

defeat, disparagement, or deprivation. Life to him is filled with burdens, heartaches, and obstacles. Negative thinking leads to depression, which in turn incites more negative thinking, thus deepening and reinforcing the depression.

A person with *a negative view of the world* believes that his experiences are demeaning. As a result, his experiences lower his already-impoverished self-image. Even neutral experiences are interpreted negatively. A neutral attitude of a friend is interpreted as rejection. A neutral comment is taken as a hostile remark. His thinking pattern is clouded by incorrect interpretations which he attaches to the behavior of other people. These interpretations are manufactured from his previously made negative conclusions about the world. He makes assumptions and generalizations, and magnifies situations out of proportion. His negative mind-set leads him to automatically make negative interpretations of situations. Defeat becomes his byword.

A depression-prone professor was given a new responsibility in his department. His first reaction was, "I'll never be able to do this." The new task was an impossibility to him. Looking in his desk for a pen he knew he had put there that morning, he began to think, "I'll never find it," even though he had only been looking for a few seconds. Every minor problem became overwhelming. When he returned home that night, he discovered that a dog had rummaged through the garbage cans and distributed the mess all over the driveway. His reaction was that the mess was too much to clean up by himself and so he left it. The situation was hopeless! He was not lazy—he actually felt inadequate to cope with the problem at hand. People with feelings of severe hopelessness and depression are *capable* of doing the job. However, they underestimate themselves and think of themselves as a total failure.

The person with a negative world view, in addition to feeling defeated, believes he is deprived. The depressed person interprets a minor event as a great loss. A young man pulled into the parking lot at church on his way to see his pastor. Just as he pulled in, another car got in his way and stalled for a few seconds. His first thought was, "I am losing valuable time which can never be made up." He went into the office and had to wait alone for ten minutes. Again he was disturbed because no one else was in the office and he was deprived of the companionship of other people.

The person with a negative world view often considers the expenditure of money, even for relatively inexpensive services such as a bus ride or telephone call, as a great loss imposed upon him by other people.

*Self-depreciation* is the second negative thinking pattern in the depressive triad. The person who has a negative view of himself constantly devalues himself regardless of circumstances. Like the person with a negative world view, he usually attaches incorrect interpretations to events.

A self-depreciating person standing in line to enter a bus believes that someone who crowds in front of him is thinking, "He's the sort of person I can do that to and get away with it." A young woman sitting in a class where she rarely speaks thinks, "I bet they think I'm stupid because I don't say anything." If she does speak, she thinks, "They must think I talk too much." In both situations she is downgrading herself. The impossible manner in which a self-depreciating person views himself leaves him with no way out.

The third thinking pattern of the depressive triad is characterized by *hopelessness regarding life and the future.* The person who thinks in this manner believes that if he is a failure now he will always be a failure. If he doesn't have a girl friend now he never will. If his marriage is unhappy now there will be no change and he is doomed to suffer for the rest of his life. This negative thinking pattern is not the same as that which occurs in the mind of one who is afraid of the future. Some people worry about things occurring. The depressed person does not worry about their occurrence; he knows that these events will take place. But he thinks the future is futile and therefore sees no reason for trying. If he does try, his effort is made in such a way that it makes defeat almost certain. This defeat in turn reinforces the original belief that the situation is hopeless.

## The Mind-Set

One of the greatest hindrances to building a positive self-concept is the mind-set. This means that a person views a situation in a preset manner, regardless of the circumstances. A person with a mind-set perceives what he *expects* to perceive. He is certain that someone is going to reject or avoid him.

Because of this certainty in his mind he begins looking for this rejection. He interprets a neutral comment as rejection. Lacking objectivity and pushing ahead with blinders on are characteristics of people with a negative mind-set. A negative mind-set can lead to serious and detrimental consequences. In *Creative and Critical Thinking*, W. Edgar Moore writes:

> The damage a mind-set can do is dramatically illustrated by the sinking of the *Titanic* on her maiden voyage in 1912, with the loss of 1513 lives. Designed to be the safest ship afloat, the *Titanic* was equipped with a double bottom and sixteen watertight compartments. A mind-set that she was unsinkable seems to have been largely responsible for the disaster.
>
> She carried lifeboats sufficient for only one-third of her capacity, and no assignment of passengers was made to these boats; nor were any drills held. The *Titanic* was unsinkable.
>
> Three days out of Queenstown, she

received her first wireless warning of icebergs in the steamer lanes. A few hours later she received another message about icebergs, but the wireless operator was too busy with his accounts to bother recording the message. The *Titanic* was unsinkable.

That afternoon another warning was received. This time the operator sent it to the Captain, who glanced at it casually and handed it without comment to the managing director of the White Star Line. By 9:30 that night at least five warnings of icebergs had been received, and the *Titanic* was nearing their reported location. But no precautions were taken other than to warn the lookouts to be alert. The owners wanted a speed record; the *Titanic* steamed ahead into the darkness at twenty-two knots. The *Titanic* was unsinkable.

She had yet another chance. At 11:30 P.M. the wireless crackled with a message from the *Californian:* "Say, old man, we are stuck here, surrounded by ice." But the mind-set held, and the *Titanic*'s operator replied, "Shut up, shut up, keep out. I am talking to Cape Race; you are jamming my signals." The *Titanic* steamed ahead at twenty-two knots; she was unsinkable.

Ten minutes later the lookout spotted

giant iceberg dead ahead. Officers on the bridge did what they could to avoid the crash, but it was too late. The collision ripped a hundred-yard gash in the ship's double bottom. Although the watertight doors were closed immediately, the bulkheads not already damaged gave way, one by one. The great ship was doomed.

The loading of the lifeboats went slowly and badly, in part because the passengers would not believe that so safe a ship could sink. The boats left the ship with nearly five hundred passengers less than capacity. At best there would have been room for no more than a thousand. Even so the casualties might have been few. Distress calls were sent out within minutes after the collision, and the ship did not sink until more than two hours later. A number of ships raced to the scene, in spite of the ice. But they were too far away to save the fifteen hundred who did not get into the lifeboats. Meantime, the *Californian* was lying within sight of the *Titanic,* possibly no more than five miles away. Her radio operator did not hear the *Titanic*'s wireless calls; he had gone to bed shortly after being told to "shut up." Some of her crew did see the *Titanic*'s lights and rocket signals but did nothing more than try to communicate with the unknown ship by blinker.

Testimony in the investigation of the disaster showed that the sea was calm and the night clear, and that the *Californian* might easily have pushed through the ice field to rescue most if not all of the passengers.

Perhaps her officers, too, had a mind-set.[1]

Do you have mind-sets? Do you anticipate how people will respond? Do you assume rejection?

The self-depreciating person dislikes himself because he feels inferior. But his inferiority complex is the result of self-rejection. When he is depressed he criticizes himself and thinks he is to blame for all of his difficulty.

Some people spend much of their life struggling to overcome feelings of inferiority. But *all* of us are inferior. We are *all* imperfect! Can you accept and enjoy your humanity? To be truly human is to live your life to the fullest by God's grace, accepting every blemish and imperfection. Greatness does not come from superior, perfect people. All of us are inferior in some way.

Did you ever see a picture of Napoleon? He was not a man of great stature, but was so short that he was jokingly called "the little corporal." One of the greatest presidents, Abraham Lincoln, was tall and gangly, with a big nose and a wart on his face; most people would agree that he was physically ugly. Franklin D. Roosevelt could not walk in his later years. Did you know that Albert Einstein had scholastic difficulties in his early years and almost failed in school?

Beethoven was an outstanding composer, but what else do you know about him? Physically, he had protruding teeth and a pockmarked face. He appeared to have a constant scowl on his face. His father was a drunk and his mother died when he was quite young. Ludwig Beethoven couldn't handle money and had a bad temper. Deafness began when he was only 30, and yet some of his greatest music was written after he became deaf.

Was Paul the Apostle great by the world's standards? From what we know of him, he was physically unattractive. Second Corinthians 10:10 suggests that his speech was contemptible and his bodily presence "unimpressive."

There will always be someone with more ability than you have, but *you* have certain qualities and strengths which *they* do not have.

*All* of us have defects and are inadequate in some way. Which do we concentrate on—the inadequacies, or the strengths and abilities that God has given us? When will we begin to see ourselves as God sees us?

*Chapter Six*

# Develop a Positive Self-Image

How can a person accept himself after years of putting himself down and even hating himself? Is it possible to go back and undo all of those hurts and rejections? Is it really possible to rid oneself of these negative feelings?

We cannot undo the past, but we *can* learn to accept what has happened in the past and put it behind us as we look to the future.

Dr. Maurice Wagner described the elements of a good self-concept in his excellent book *The Sensation of Being Somebody*. He suggests that there are three kinds of feelings that have unusual significance in forming the essential elements of self-concept: belongingness, worthiness, and competence. These three feelings constitute the mental structure of the self-concept. These three feelings support and stabilize the self-concept like the three legs of a tripod support its top. If any of the three begins to weaken, the self-concept totters.

*Belongingness* is the awareness of being wanted, accepted, cared for, and enjoyed. Are you aware of being wanted? By whom? Are you accepted? By whom? How do you know? Do others enjoy you? Do you enjoy yourself? How do you know?

*Worthiness* is a feeling of "I am good," "I count," and "I am all right." People feel worthy when they do what they think they should. This feeling is verified when we sense that other people have positive attitudes toward us. We look for their endorsement of our actions. A feeling of worthiness is related to a sense of being right and doing right in our eyes and in the eyes of other people. Belongingness and worthiness are similar. A person feels good about himself when accepted by others. When do you feel most worthy? What do you have to feel worthy about? Who else sees you as worthy?

*Competence* is a feeling of adequacy. It is the feeling "I can," "I have the ability or strength to do it." A feeling of adequacy is built upon present as well as past accomplishments. It is based upon the achievement of goals and ideals that we have for ourself. When do you feel most adequate? Who else sees you as adequate? List several positive things you have accomplished. What are your personal strengths?

Before reading further in this book, complete the following sentence ten times. Write your first response each time you read it.

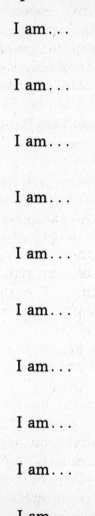

I am...

I am...

I am...

I am...

I am...

I am...

I am...

I am...

I am...

I am...

Now read back through your responses. Are they positive or negative? You weren't asked to give all negative or all positive statements, so this may be a good indication of how you feel about yourself. If most of your responses are negative, think about them and write a positive response in place of each negative one. Sometimes a person writes all negative statements. When asked to substitute a positive statement for a negative one, he may deny that there is anything positive about himself. He may say, "It would be impossible for me to do that. There isn't anything positive about me. I can't do anything. I'm really worthless."

A closer look, however, reveals that there are positive things in his life. Even getting out of bed, dressing oneself, and fixing breakfast are positive steps, for there are many people who cannot do even that.

Dr. Wagner describes how these three elements—belongingness, worthiness, and competence—together form the self-concept.

> Belongingness is fundamental. Worthiness somewhat depends on belongingness, for one must feel accepted by others to value their confirming attitudes concerning how good a person he is. Competence depends partially on belongingness and upon worthiness. We need to feel accepted by others in order to value their approval or profit by their helpful criticism. We also must

approve of ourselves to have the incentive to keep trying after we have failed. We tend to become listless and apathetic when we lose our sense of worthiness and feel like a non-person, depressed.

Reviewing the essential nature of these three feelings, we observe these facts: Belongingness rests on the voluntary attitude of others as they display their acceptance. Worthiness rests on the introspective attitude of self-approval. Competence rests on the evaluations received in past relationships and on one's present sense of success.

Note that belongingness positions a person with respect to other people. Belongingness gives an orientation in society as "one of them." One has the underlying feeling of being either "in" or "out" with people.

Worthiness positions a person with respect to his own ideals and conduct. It gives him an orientation with respect to the appropriateness of his behavior. He is aware of being either good or bad, worth something or nothing.

Competence positions a person with respect to life situations. It is related to how he copes with life. Competence orients a person to circumstances, to time, to responsibility, to usefulness, and to fulfillment in his role in life.

These three feelings work together to give a person a sense of identity, a self-orientation to living. Belongingness, worthiness, and competence are essential elements of self-concept and together they affirm to a person that he is somebody.[1]

How can we develop a sense of belongingness? How can we be worthy? How can we have a feeling of competence?

The first step in the process of developing a healthy self-image is to *seek a personal relationship with Jesus Christ.* Someone may say, "Do you mean that the only way I can have a good self-image is to become a Christian? I know some Christians who don't like themselves and are no example of a person who has a good self-concept. And I know some others who aren't Christians who seem like they have a good self-concept." It is possible for a non-Christian to have a good self-image. But a person who knows Jesus Christ not only has a greater opportunity for developing a healthy self-image but also has a means for developing his self-image to its fullest!

When a man opens himself to God, he begins to see himself in proper perspective and begins to know himself as he really is. Through Jesus Christ he discovers the healing of his defects. When a person experiences the unconditional acceptance of God, he gains the courage to open himself up to other people and begins to overcome his fear of rejection. Sometimes this relationship begins because of seeing Christ in another person's life. Another person's acceptance may show us God's acceptance.

The masks and facades that we have worn for years are slowly removed in God's presence as we find that He accepts us and loves us—faults and all! God helps us shed these masks in our relationships with other people. In the process we begin to discover ourselves and relate to others.

If we continue through life without accepting Christ, we continue to focus upon a distorted self-image. Man was originally created in the image of God, but this image was distorted with the fall of man. When we accept Christ, He enables us to see the image of God in us. Being fully aware of God's image in us is a critical step in understanding ourselves and in discovering our real identity. Most people look at others around them or to the future to help establish their identity, but we can look to God for our identity. When a person becomes a Christian he becomes aware of being somebody. We are somebody to God! That is significant.

Roger sat in my office, head down, staring at the floor. He kept saying, "Just one person, just one person. All I ask for is one person...."

I said, "Just one person who will—"

"One person who will believe in me. No one believes in me," Roger replied. Roger was in a trap. He didn't believe in himself, he lacked confidence, and he failed in most of what he attempted. This caused other people to become angry with him and dump on him which further eroded his confidence and caused his self-esteem to sink even lower.

All of us need someone to believe in us. It encourages us to believe in ourselves. But other people are hesitant to believe in us if we don't seem to believe in ourselves.

Do you know what the good news is? Someone believes in you. God believes in you. The One who believes in you is the One who has asked you to believe in Him.

He doesn't compare you with the other people He has created. He has given you your own capabilities and potential. He expects you to develop and use only what He has given you, not what He has given someone else. He wants you to develop and use what you have so you won't miss out on life. You are God's workmanship:

> For we are His workmanship, created
> in Christ Jesus for good works, which
> God prepared beforehand, that we
> should walk in them (Ephesians 2:10).

Jesus Christ invites us to come to Him by faith, believing that He will accept us as we are into His family:

> But as many as received Him, to them
> He gave the right to become children
> of God, even to those who believe in
> His name, who were born not of blood,

nor of the will of the flesh, nor of the
will of man, but of God (John 1:12,13).

Dr. Wagner suggests that when we have the
assurance of being someone because of God's
unconditional love, we can then disregard the
idea that we are nobody. We know that we are
somebody to God! Our relationships with other
people can now be put on a different plane. We
can love others because we have been loved. We
can learn to love unconditionally because we
have been loved unconditionally. We have been
accepted with an unconditional acceptance even
though we are imperfect. Therefore we can learn
to forgive the faults and defects in others. Second Corinthians 5:17 states, "Therefore if any
man is in Christ, he is a new creature; the old
things passed away; behold, new things have
come." We are God's new creation—we are His
workmanship. The One who had the only
perfect self-concept, Jesus Christ, is now our
model. Our sense of being somebody comes
through our relationship with Him. Paul told us,
"Put on the new self, who is being renewed to
a true knowledge according to the image of the
One who created him" (Colossians 3:10).

How does a relationship with God fulfill these
three self-image pillars of belongingness, worthiness, and competence? Because of our position
in Christ, we know that we are accepted by God.
We belong to Him: "He hath made us accepted
in the beloved" (Ephesians 1:6 KJV). Because
God has forgiven our sins, we can say that we

are good. "Therefore having been justified by faith, we have peace with God through our Lord Jesus Christ" (Romans 5:1). If God and Jesus Christ are with us at all times, we know we are not inferior or inadequate. God is our source of adequacy. We can love ourselves without pangs of guilt. We can love ourselves without having to defend our actions.

A Christian should love himself because God loves him. God loves people and wants to reconcile them to Himself. Sinful people are valuable to God. If God loves sinful people for the redeemable value He sees in them, then we ought to love these people too, including ourselves.

Dr. Lloyd Ahlem in *Do I Have to Be Me?* so clearly summarizes what God has done for us.

> The writers of the Scriptures are careful to point out that when God looks at you in Jesus Christ, He sees you as a brother to His own Son. . . . You are worth all of God's attention. If you were the only person in the world, it would be worth God's effort to make Himself known to you and to love you. He gives you freely the status and adequacy of an heir to the universe.[2]

This gift has been offered to each and every person. Our part is to accept the gift. This means that we begin to live a life of faith. Our self-concept is based on the fact of what God has done, and we accept it by faith. This also means that we must challenge some of our built-in attitudes and feelings. Man cannot and must not live by feelings, but by faith.

Unfortunately, many people cannot accept this free gift from God, and they cannot accept a gift of love from other people either. Ahlem continues:

> We insist on bartering when He [God] would give us His gifts freely. He offers us forgiveness, status, adequacy, direction in life. Instead of responding with thanks and love, we insist on earning the gift or trading something for it. We become so religious nobody can stand us. Or we refuse his gift and say that we do not deserve it. Or we become so aseptically moral that no needy human can touch us. We forget so quickly that Jesus was the one who took care of any shortage of payment we owe, or any bartering that had to be done; He gave Himself so that we could freely receive. You can be adequate. You can be guilt-free! Accept His love; your doubts about the truth of the matter will vanish when you do. He will put His spirit within you, and honest joy will surprise you.

When a person has accepted adequacy as a gift, he immediately perceives a new standard for achievement. No longer does the criterion of human performance apply, but rather the measure of faithfulness judges us. This is the fair standard, the one that stimulates everyone, frustrates no one, and is administered by the providential will of God.[3]

The second step in the process of developing a healthy self-image is to *accept the truth of the Scriptures.* The Word of God is the base upon which we build a positive feeling about ourselves. The Scriptures teach us in Proverbs 23:7 that what a man thinks in his heart is manifested in his life. If we begin to think positively about ourselves, the change in our thinking will appear in our behavior.

Even though you have probably suffered from feelings of inadequacy, by fully receiving God's love and acceptance you can believe that you are worthwhile. Read, reread, and study the following verses of Scripture until you know them by memory. *Believe* that they are speaking about you. *Accept* them by faith!

Therefore having been justified by faith, we have peace with God through our Lord Jesus Christ (Romans 5:1).

There is therefore now no condemnation for those who are in Christ Jesus.... The Spirit Himself bears witness with our spirit that we are children of God, and if children, heirs also, heirs of God and fellow-heirs with

Christ, if indeed we suffer with Him in order that we may also be glorified with Him (Romans 8:1,16,17).

You might be tempted to say, "Well, I don't *feel* justified," or, "I don't *feel* that I'm not condemned." But feelings cannot be relied upon because they fluctuate and are not always dependable. Instead, ask yourself, "If I really did believe these verses, how would I be feeling and how would I be acting?" After you have answered this question, begin to act as you have decided you would if these verses were a part of your life. If you change your actions, you will soon find that your feelings are also changing.

The third step in the process of developing a healthy self-image is to *begin practicing openness and honesty with yourself and others.* The starting point for a life of honesty and disclosure begins with your relationship with God. Begin acknowledging to God your personal struggles, doubts, and betrayals. Confession of sin is an essential condition for spiritual and psychological health and a positive self-image. But too much concentration upon sins can become a morbid and unhealthy pastime, especially if the sins are in the past and have been confessed, forgiven, and forsaken. Paul admonished his readers, "Forgetting what lies behind and straining forward to what lies ahead, I press on" (Philippians 3:13,14 RSV).

If you have struggled with a poor self-concept for years, you may have the tendency to overemphasize and dwell upon sin in your life.

The Scriptures depict the inner turmoil of those who try to cover their sin:

> When I declared not my sin, my body wasted away through my groaning all day long. For day and night thy hand was heavy upon me; my strength was dried up as by the heat of summer.
>
> I acknowledged my sin to thee, and I did not hide my iniquity; I said, "I will confess my transgressions to the Lord;" then thou didst forgive the guilt of my sin (Psalm 32:3-5 RSV).

Sin cannot be hidden. Jesus said there are no secrets we can keep from God:

> Nothing is covered up that will not be revealed, or hidden that will not be known. Therefore whatever you have said in the dark shall be heard in the light, and what you have whispered in private rooms shall be proclaimed upon the housetops (Luke 12:2,3 RSV).

The purpose of confession of sin is two-fold, as expressed in Proverbs 28:13: "He who conceals his transgressions will not prosper, but he who confesses and forsakes them will obtain mercy" (RSV). Forgiveness and forsaking are inseparable.

The Psalms illustrate that forgiveness of sin occurs when confession is made. This covering or blotting out of sin is accomplished solely by God, not by us:

> Blessed is he whose transgression is
> forgiven, whose sin is covered.... I
> acknowledged my sin to thee, and I did
> not hide my iniquity; I said, "I will con-
> fess my transgressions to the Lord";
> then thou didst forgive the guilt of my
> sin (Psalm 32:1,5 RSV).

The Scriptures say that God Himself blots out our sins. He casts them behind His back, buries them, and remembers them no more. If we bring known sins out into the open with shame and remorse, God forgives them. We do not have to allow sins to linger in our life anymore. If God has forgiven and forgotten them, then who are we to retain a hold on them? This freedom from past sin is further proof that we are of tremendous value to God. Our worth and value is shown by the fact that if we had been the only person here on earth, God still would have sent His Son to die for our sins.

The fourth step in this process is to *understand and apply the Scriptural teaching about our thought life.* Thought patterns can be changed. The Scriptures promise that negative thinking can be changed to positive thinking.

Ephesians 4:23 states that we are to be renewed in the spirit of our minds. The Scripture is referring here to a mind controlled by the Holy Spirit. Renewal is an act of God's Spirit influencing the spirit of man—his mental attitude or state of mind. Paul said in Romans 12:2, "Do not be conformed to this world, but be transformed by the renewing of your mind." He is talking about a renovation, a complete change for the better. The word *renewal* means "to make new from above." Through the process of renewal, a man's thoughts, imaginations, and reasonings can be changed through the working of the Holy Spirit.

## Controlling Your Thoughts

The process involved in controlling your thoughts is to *allow the Holy Spirit to work in your own life.* The key is your willingness to let the Holy Spirit accomplish His purpose in you. Renewal of the mind brings about a spiritual transformation in the life of the Christian.

Then *consider the direction of your thought life.* What do you think about? As suggested by Proverbs 23:7, as a man "thinks within himself, so he is." As we build up storehouses of memories, knowledge, and experiences, we seem to retain and remember those things which we concentrate upon the most. If we concentrate upon rejection and hurt, they will be a part of our experience. Each person is responsible for the things he allows his mind to dwell upon. We are told in Philippians 4:8 what we are to think about:

> Finally, brethren, whatever is true, whatever is honorable, whatever is just, whatever is pure, whatever is lovely, whatever is gracious, if there

is any excellence, if there is anything
worthy of praise, think about these
things (RSV).

Colossians 3:2 advises that we should set our
minds and keep them set on what is above—
the higher things—not on the things that are on
the earth.

Whenever we experience tumors of doubt
about our worth, they must be removed. When
the beginnings of self-contempt start to release
their poison, they must be stopped immediately.

We must also *realize that the Christian does not
have to be dominated by the thinking of the old
mind,* which in many cases is a negative mind-
set. "For God hath not given us the spirit of fear,
but of power, and of love, and of a sound mind"
(2 Timothy 1:7 KJV). Soundness means that the
new mind can do what it is supposed to do. It
can fulfill its function.

Another way to control your thoughts is to *let
your mind be filled with the mind of Christ.* Three
Scripture passages place definite responsibility
upon the Christian in this regard. In Philippians
2:5 Paul commands, "Let this mind be in you,
which was also in Christ Jesus" (KJV). This could
be translated, "Be constantly thinking this in
yourselves," or, "Reflect in your own minds the
mind of Christ Jesus." The meaning here of the
words *this mind be* is "to have understanding,
to be wise, to direct one's mind to a thing, to
seek or strive for."

A second passage, 1 Peter 1:13, tells us, "Gird

your minds for action." The words refer to mental exertion, putting out of the mind anything that would hinder progress in the Christian experience. Thoughts of worry, fear, negative interpretations, and unforgiveness are to be eliminated from the mind. It is *our* responsibility to eliminate them and replace them with positive thoughts. It takes effort, determination, and a desire to do this. But when the desire is there, the ministry of the Holy Spirit is available to assist us. Often the process is best accomplished by first bringing in the positive thoughts.[4]

Herman Gockel writes about this process in *Answer to Anxiety* and suggests:

> There is much more to this whole business than merely getting rid of negative or unworthy thoughts. In fact, the concept of "getting rid" is itself a sign of negative thinking. We shall succeed in this whole matter, not in the measure in which we empty our minds of sinful and degrading thoughts, but rather in the measure in which we *fill* them with thoughts that are wholesome and uplifting. The human mind can never be a vacuum. He who thinks he can improve the tenants of his soul simply by evicting those that are unworthy will find that for every unworthy tenant he evicts through the back door, several more will enter through the front (see Matthew

12:43-45). It is not merely a matter of evicting. It is also a matter of screening, selecting, admitting, and cultivating those tenants that have proved themselves desirable.[5]

Philippians 4:6-8 tells us what to *stop* thinking about and what to *begin* thinking about:

Be anxious for nothing, but in everything by prayer and supplication with thanksgiving let your requests be made known to God. And the peace of God, which surpasses all comprehension, shall guard your hearts and your minds in Christ Jesus. Finally brethren, whatever is true, whatever is honorable, whatever is right, whatever is pure, whatever is lovely, whatever is of good repute, if there is any excellence and if anything worthy of praise, let your mind dwell on these things.

*Chapter Seven*

# Self-Talk

We become upset and reinforce our poor image of ourselves by what is called self-talk. Every person talks to himself. For some, the messages are positive, but for others they are always negative. When someone fails to speak to us in a group, we begin talking to ourselves: "I wonder why John didn't say hello. Oh, well, perhaps he still has a lot on his mind. He's been having some rough times lately. And he probably has a number of other people to see while he's here. I'll catch him another time or else I'll give him a call." This person handled the situation positively and objectively. But another person begins a line of self-talk: "I wonder why he didn't speak to me. Maybe he doesn't want to talk to me. Maybe he doesn't like me or there are other more important people here to see. I wonder if I've offended him in some way." Negative self-talk leads to a poor self-image.

A man gives a speech at a meeting, but it doesn't go over too well. There are two basic styles of self-talk which he can employ. The positive style says: "Well, that speech wasn't too good. I have to give another one next week, so I think I better spend twice as long preparing for it. I think I'll practice it out loud in front of the mirror and with a tape recorder. I'll ask my wife to listen to it and get her opinion." A negative style of self-talk might be: "That was a rotten speech. How can I face those people? They must think I'm a clod. That will ruin my business. I'll never get the promotion. What if my supervisor gets feedback on this presentation? He may not even want me to work for him. I'll try to find a way to slip out of this meeting early."

When asked why she was depressed and upset, a young lady replied that her boyfriend had rejected her. She thought the rejection was causing the depression. However, that was not entirely true. Her *subjective interpretation* of his rejection was the real cause. "It's awful to be rejected like that," she thinks. "I'm deeply hurt. Why did this happen to me? It shouldn't happen to me. I must be a failure. I'm also unattractive. There must be something wrong with me."

Messages and thoughts like these are the factors bringing on the depression. Statements like "It shouldn't happen to me; I must be a failure; I'm unattractive" are neither rational nor true. No one is immune to rejection at all times in his life. Just because it happened doesn't mean that the person is unattractive or a failure! Irrational messages such as these bring about the emotional reaction of depression. It is normal for a person to be upset and sad when a relationship is broken, but not to that extent. It would be better for this girl to think rationally, "I'm sad because of this situation and I wish it could have worked out. I'll miss him. This is unfortunate, but it's not the end of the world." In most cases it is not the event or circumstance that brings about an emotional reaction but our *interpretation of it*.

Montaigne wrote, "A man is hurt not so much by what happens as by his opinion of what happens." In *The Encheiridion*, Epictetus observed, "Men are disturbed not by things but by the views which they take of them." Shakespeare expressed this thought in *Hamlet*: "There is nothing either good or bad, but thinking makes it so." Vincent Collins, in *Me, Myself and You*, suggests, "It is not our situation that makes us happy or miserable; it's the way in which we react to it."

Some people operate under a set of misbeliefs which cause them to continually deny themselves and always seek to please others. Their misbeliefs reflect a poor self-image and keep them from developing in a positive direction. Here are some typical misbeliefs:

- The way to be liked by other people is to be what others want me to be and to do what is most pleasing to them.

- It is more Christian to please other people than to please myself.

- Other people have the right to judge my actions.

- It is wrong and unchristian to think my own needs are important when compared to the needs of others.

- It is wrong not to forget my own wants in order to please friends and family when they want me to.

- Pleasing others is an insurance policy which guarantees that people will be nice to me in return. When I am in great need they will forget their own needs and help me.

- When other people are displeased with me, it is impossible to get one moment's peace or happiness.

- Approval from everyone else is absolutely necessary to my feelings of well-being and peace of mind, since God doesn't want me to be happy unless everyone else is approving of me.

- Being what other people want me to be is the only way to be liked.

- Pleasing others and doing what they expect of me is the only way to win friends.

By contrast, here are some beliefs and thoughts which are positive, balanced, and healthy:

- It is *not* necessary to be liked by everyone.

- I do not have to earn anyone's approval or acceptance to be a person of worth.

- I am a child of God. I m deeply loved by Him, and I have been forgiven by Him; therefore I am acceptable. I accept myself.

- My needs and wants are as important as other people's.

- Rejection is *not* terrible. It may be a bit unpleasant, but it is not terrible.

- Not being approved or accepted is *not* terrible. It may not be desirable, but it is not terrible.

- If somebody doesn't like me, I can live with it. I don't have to work feverishly to get him/her to like me.

- I can conquer my bad feelings by distinguishing the truth from misbelief.

- It is a misbelief that I must please other people and be approved by them.

- Jesus died on the cross for me so that I

can be free from the misbelief that other people decide my value.

Pleasing others is a principle which could be directly opposed to the basic rule of the Christian's life: *to please God.* God's will for you may be at variance with other people's claims, demands, and whims. God's will for Jesus, for example, was contrary to the demands of the multitude, who wanted to make Him king after He fed 5000 people with the little boy's meager lunch (John 6).

Frequently, God's will for you will require that you consider your own needs first and set aside the wishes of others. There were times when Jesus put His own needs for rest and food ahead of ministering to other people. If you try to neglect yourself and your own needs (unless you are under direct instructions from the Lord), you will encounter spiritual and psychological troubles. Being cruel to yourself is not necessarily "holy."

In making judgments about what you should do, it is too simplistic to base these on the rule "Whatever pleases other people must be right." The critical needs of another human being will very likely often be given precedence over your own plans and less critical needs—at times even your own crucial needs. But there are other times when your own needs will take precedence.

If you live to please others, any negative feedback criticism, or displeasure will tend to ruin

you. You actually set yourself up for distur-
bance, for it will disturb you to think that other
people are not perfectly happy with you. You
must learn to take criticism and handle it as a
"very small thing," to quote Paul, who knew
that it was the Lord who was the true judge (1
Corinthians 4:3).

Even if nearly everyone disliked you and
disapproved of you, you could still survive. Jesus
did. Many others have managed to live through
large amounts of disapproval by other people.
If you are willing to take God at His Word, "I
will not leave you nor forsake you" (see
Hebrews 13:5), there is no reason to believe that
you will collapse or disintegrate when others
disapprove of you. Of course, the displeasure of
others is often unpleasant for us to tolerate, and
it may be very difficult to endure, especially
when those who are important to us do not approve of us. Nevertheless, if we have to, we can
stand it. And most of the time disapproval by
other people is short-lived and restricted. It is
very unlikely that we will encounter a circumstance where absolutely *everyone* will dislike
us and disapprove of us.[1]

There are several steps which you can take to
change the direction of your self-talk. Remember
that the two main reasons that Christians can
change their self-talk are 1) we have the ministry
of the Holy Spirit working in our lives, and 2)
we can respond to the Scriptural basis for our
thinking pattern.

Life will always have some unpleasant situations. The Bible tells us to expect them, but it also gives us the basic attitude we can have toward them: "Consider it all joy, my brethren, when you encounter various trials, knowing that the testing of your faith produces endurance" (James 1:2,3).

The first step in the process of changing self-talk is to *state very precisely the unpleasant situation that you have experienced.* Most unpleasant situations involve our own or someone else's failure or mistakes, or an unfortunate set of circumstances. To more clearly identify what you are upset about, ask these questions.

1. Am I upsetting myself over some real mistake or error that I have made?

2. Am I upset or discouraged because of another person's behavior? (For example, my husband is not being what I think he should be, my child is not behaving as I desire, or my boss is being unfair to me.)

3. Am I feeling bad because of an unfortunate set of circumstances?

The second step in this process is to *list or identify what it is that you are saying to yourself about the situation.* Most people begin talking to themselves about how awful the situation is or about the things that should have happened.

When a college student fails a course, what should he tell himself upon receiving news of the failure? He may feel that he should receive all "As" or "Bs" in his courses. He may feel that he has ruined his chance for graduate study or even for graduating from college. Other thoughts might include: "If other people know about this, they will really think I'm stupid. I must be an idiot. I'll never succeed at anything in my life. This could ruin my chances at getting a good job when I do get out of school."

The third step in this process of changing your self-talk is to *challenge your self-talk*. When you challenge your self-talk, you check the facts—the evidence—that led you to the conclusion that the situation is so awful.

The college student who failed a course could ask himself some of these questions:

1. What rational basis do I have for telling myself that my chances of going to graduate school are ruined? Is it possible that the failing of one course will prevent me from going to graduate school?

2. What is the evidence that other people will think I'm stupid? Can I read other people's minds to know what they're thinking? Why wouldn't people think I'm simply fallible like everyone else? They have probably experienced some failure in their own life, so they know how I feel.

3. What basis do I have for telling myself that I'll never succeed at anything? I succeeded in graduating from grade school and from high school and in passing many college courses. I know I can succeed. Look at all the other successes I've had in my life.

4. Who says I should get "As" and "Bs" in all

my courses? I'm a fallible human being. Should I expect to be a perfect student?

Here is another approach to challenging your self-talk.[2]

**SITUATION:** Mary is unhappy because someone she is very close to is graduating and going off to college in another state.

**NEGATIVE THOUGHT:** I should be happy all the time. Christians should not be unhappy.

**RESULTING FEELINGS:** Unworthiness, shame.

**RESULTING BEHAVIOR:** Mary does not express to her friend that she will miss her. Her friend gets the impression that Mary doesn't care that she's leaving.

**COUNTERS** (arguments against the negative thought):

1. That's nonsense! I can't think of one Biblical character who was happy all the time!

2. That negative thought is a great way to lose friends fast!

3. That's dumb! I'm trying to be God.

4. Whoever told me that Christians should never be unhappy? Certainly my pastor has never suggested it!

5. (You add one) _____

6. (Another) _____

**SITUATION:** Jim is sitting alone in his home.

Several things have gone wrong for him this week, and he would like to be able to get some support from someone. He starts to tell his family what has happened, but hesitates again and again.

**NEGATIVE THOUGHT:** Strong people don't ask for help.

**RESULTING FEELINGS:** Extreme loneliness, dejection.

**RESULTING BEHAVIOR:** Jim stays in his apartment all weekend. He even gets drunk.

**COUNTERS:**

1. Moses asked for help from God continually. He asked God for help to be able to speak to the Israelites. And Moses became one of the greatest leaders Israel ever had.
2. Other people I know ask for help continually.
3. I often help other people with their problems. Am I not entitled to the same?
4. It's okay not to be perfect.
5. This thought only hurts me.
6. (Your turn!) _____
7. (Again) _____

## How to Identify Your Basic Negative Beliefs

1. Become aware of your automatic thoughts. Your automatic thoughts rest on implicit beliefs. Although these beliefs may be silent, they can be inferred from the thoughts that lead to bad feelings. When Mrs. Jones's boss ignored her,

she thought, "He doesn't like me." This was based on her belief that "Everyone has to like me all the time."

2. Look for themes. Look over your automatic thoughts. See how many are of a particular type. You'll see a pattern forming in your thinking ("I'm dumb," "I'm ugly," "Nobody loves me," "I'm too old"). Note situations in which you frequently feel bad. For one person, Janice, these situations often revolved around rejection and standards of personal appearance: "Everyone has to accept (love) me," and "People have to think I'm attractive." These general themes were part of her basic underlying beliefs: "People won't love you if you're ugly." Ugly to her applied not only to appearance but also to personality. Her belief could go in a number of different directions ("I'm unhappy, so that means I must be an ugly person"; "I have to fool people to make them think I'm attractive"; "I'll be ugly when I get old, so I'll be unhappy").

3. Note key words. You may find that you use the same words over and over again in your automatic thoughts—words such as rotten, weird, ugly. These are clues to your underlying beliefs. Because most of your beliefs were learned when you were a child, they contain words that children use (such as stupid and dumb).

Once these words have been identified, uncover the meanings behind them. This is the time to sit back and reflect on your childhood. Certain family sayings and bedtime stories may contain further clues.

Janice often used the word "ugly" in her negative thoughts. Thinking back to her childhood, she remembered her relatives saying that her sister was the pretty one and that Janice was the one with the brains. She identified with the ugly-duckling story.

4. See how you view other people. Another clue to your underlying beliefs is the way you see others. This requires identifying your thinking even more. For example, Jean thought, "Shannon has lots of dates because she's beautiful." Also look for people with whom you feel the most uncomfortable. What is it about them that gets to you? Jean didn't like extremely attractive women.

5. Underline thinking errors. Look over your automatic thoughts and see what kinds of errors you make the most. Overgeneralizing? Jumping to conclusions? Ignoring the positive? Thinking in either/or and all-or-nothing terms? Here are some examples.

| All-or-Nothing Thinking | Realistic Thinking |
| --- | --- |
| A. I'm a complete failure. | A. I've succeeded at some things and failed at others. So I think I'll rejoin the human race. Does God think I'm a failure? Hardly. Would He bother to die for me if I were worthless? |

B. I'm too old.

B. Too old for what? Too old to have a good time? No. Too old for sex? No. Too old to learn? No. Too old to love? No. Too old to enjoy music? No. Then what am I too old for?

C. People don't like me.

C. I've never heard anyone say that. I have several friends who call me each week. They would not call if they hated me. I was asked at church to serve as a deacon. Someone must like me.

D. I can't get over this habit. Therefore, I am not a Christian. I must be lost.

D. Where does it say in Scripture that I must break all my bad habits in order to be saved? I'll enlist God's help to change it. I'll depend on Him to help me decrease and stop the habit.

6. Examine your happiness. When you're unusually happy about some event, ask yourself, "Why am I so happy?" Many underlying beliefs have a payoff when they appear to be working.

For example, when a man paid attention to Jean, she became exuberant. Conversely, she became depressed when she thought men weren't paying attention to her.[3]

The final step in the process of changing self-talk is a very positive one which we can use in all areas of our life: *Improve what can be improved!* After challenging our negative thoughts and bringing them into proper perspective, we can begin to plan and implement a course of action that will improve the distressing situation. This, too, is accomplished through the process of self-talk, but it is now more constructive and takes on a definite direction. For example:

> Since I failed a course in my major field of study and since it is to my advantage to pass this course, I will take it again and attempt to get at least a "C" in it. I will do this by setting aside two hours each day to complete the requirements of this course. I will get someone to tutor me and help me with my papers. If I fail the course again, TOO BAD! It is not a disaster and does not have to destroy me. I can and will have a meaningful and satisfying college experience even though I failed the course.[4]

It is possible to loosen the hold of real or apparent rejection, but it is a slow process. You may tend to become impatient. Your tendency may be to focus on some of the remaining feelings of rejection and fail to notice the improvements. Remember to focus upon the small improvements.

The process of growing is similar to that of a child learning to walk up stairs. It involves carefully putting one foot on the first step and then lifting yourself up until the second foot also rests on that step. Then you must remember to rest both feet on that step before you swing yourself up onto the next step. At each step you must repeat the process. In time you build confidence and can move more rapidly, with one foot taking one step and the other foot the next step.

To build your self-concept, you must first *give yourself acceptance.* Acceptance means that you stop downgrading yourself, belittling yourself, and berating yourself. As God puts His arms around you and tells you that you are lovable and worthwhile, you can do the same. Part of accepting yourself involves accepting the fact that although you did experience hurt in the past and those experiences cannot be changed, you can loosen the hold they have on you now. You climb one step at a time with both feet and rest there before proceeding on to the next level. At each level you give yourself reassurance and approval and reinforce your worth.

As you proceed, the next step is to *take an area of your life in which you would like to perform with more skill and begin to build and strengthen it* until you see change and growth. Even failures at this level can be considered as growth-producing experiences if we have a positive attitude.

The last step is to *fill your mind with thoughts and resources which will help you.* Scripture itself fills this need. "How can a young man keep his way pure? By guarding it according to thy word. With my whole heart I see thee; let me not wander from thy commandments! I have laid up thy word in my heart, that I might not sin against thee (Psalm 119:9-11 RSV).

We are also told to "desire the sincere milk of the word, that ye may grow by it" (1 Peter 2:2 KJV). The Word of God is the safeguard against negative thinking. Solomon said to commit your works to the Lord: "He will cause your thoughts to become agreeable to His will, and so shall your plans be established and succeed" (Proverbs 16:3 AMP).

Reading, studying, and memorizing the Word of God will make it easier to think and act according to the pattern it sets forth. Webb Garrison writes in *The Joy of Memorizing Scripture* that "a 'mind-set' is slowly molded by Scripture that is memorized and often repeated. Anyone who devotes as much as fifteen minutes a day to this process for several years undergoes subtle changes. Most of them occur so gradually that he is hardly aware of them."[5]

*Chapter Eight*

# A Self-Evaluation

The following summary will help you set goals to work toward. Work on one area of your life at a time, and you will reach the goal.

When a person has a positive self-concept:

1. He believes strongly in a set of values and principles and is willing to defend them (in the proper manner) in the face of strong opinion. He is secure enough to stand up for them or to modify them if there is adequate evidence that he is in error.

   a. Give a specific illustration of this.___

    b. What do you need to do at this time to make this a reality? _____

_____

_____

_____

2. His adequacy and identity result from his relationships with God and man. God's self-giving love has been absorbed into his life so that he is now secure and emotionally self-supporting.

    a. Give a specific illustration of this.\_\_\_\_

_____

_____

    b. What do you need to do at this time to make this a reality? _____

_____

_____

_____

3. He has a nondefensive attitude toward people. He does not make it a practice to protect his image or reputation or feelings.

    a. Give a specific illustration of this.\_\_\_\_

_____

_____

    b. What do you need to do at this time to make this a reality? _____

_____

_____

4. He is capable of acting upon his own best judgment and does not feel guilty if other people do not approve of what he has done.

   a. Give a specific illustration of this.＿

   ＿＿＿＿＿＿＿＿＿＿＿＿＿＿＿＿＿＿

   ＿＿＿＿＿＿＿＿＿＿＿＿＿＿＿＿＿＿

   b. What do you need to do at this time to make this a reality? ＿＿＿＿＿＿＿

   ＿＿＿＿＿＿＿＿＿＿＿＿＿＿＿＿＿＿

   ＿＿＿＿＿＿＿＿＿＿＿＿＿＿＿＿＿＿

   ＿＿＿＿＿＿＿＿＿＿＿＿＿＿＿＿＿＿

5. He does not spend time worrying about what will occur tomorrow or what has occurred in the past.

   a. Give a specific illustration of this.＿

   ＿＿＿＿＿＿＿＿＿＿＿＿＿＿＿＿＿＿

   ＿＿＿＿＿＿＿＿＿＿＿＿＿＿＿＿＿＿

   b. What do you need to do at this time to make this a reality? ＿＿＿＿＿＿＿

   ＿＿＿＿＿＿＿＿＿＿＿＿＿＿＿＿＿＿

   ＿＿＿＿＿＿＿＿＿＿＿＿＿＿＿＿＿＿

6. He has confidence in his ability to deal with problems even when he experiences setbacks or failures. He sees these as learning experiences (James 1:2,3).

   a. Give a specific illustration of this.＿

   ＿＿＿＿＿＿＿＿＿＿＿＿＿＿＿＿＿＿

   ＿＿＿＿＿＿＿＿＿＿＿＿＿＿＿＿＿＿

b. What do you need to do at this time to make this a reality? _____

_____

_____

_____

7. His security and identity enable him to be open with people. He sees their potential and positive qualities. He accepts them as imperfect individuals. He seeks to understand their uniqueness.

a. Give a specific illustration of this. ____

_____

_____

b. What do you need to do at this time to make this a reality? _____

_____

_____

_____

8. He feels equal to others as a person. He does not constantly evaluate himself or others on a scale of superiority and inferiority.

a. Give a specific illustration of this. ____

_____

_____

b. What do you need to do at this time to make this a reality? _____

_____

9. He can accept praise without false modesty and accept compliments without guilt. He does not go out of his way to seek the approval of other people.

   a. Give a specific illustration of this.___

   _____

   _____

   b. What do you need to do at this time to make this a reality? _____

   _____

   _____

   _____

10. He recognizes that he has worth to himself, to God, and to other people.

    a. Give a specific illustration of this.___

    _____

    _____

    b. What do you need to do at this time to make this a reality? _____

    _____

    _____

    _____

11. He accepts his emotions as a product of the way God created him.

    a. Give a specific illustration of this.___

    _____

    _____

b. What do you need to do at this time to make this a reality? _____
_____
_____
_____

12. He is sensitive to the needs of other people and realizes that he cannot enjoy himself at the expense of others.
a. Give a specific illustration of this.___
_____
_____

b. What do you need to do at this time to make this a reality? _____
_____
_____
_____

13. He seeks to apply God's example of love to other people and refrains from imposing his own judgments or stereotypes upon others.
a. Give a specific illustration of this.___
_____
_____

b. What do you need to do at this time to make this a reality? _____
_____
_____
_____

*Chapter Nine*

# Check the Scriptures

Many people have the attitude, "I'm just no good." But what does the Word of God say? Your sins are forgiven:

> And seeing their faith, He said, "Friend, your sins are forgiven you" (Luke 5:20).

Christ came to redeem sinners:

> I have not come to call the righteous but sinners to repentance (Luke 5:32).

God values each person highly:

111

I say to you, among those born of women, there is no one greater than John; yet he who is least in the kingdom of God is greater than he (Luke 7:28).

You are justified in Christ:

...that He might be just and the justifier of the one who has faith in Jesus (Romans 3:26).

God has forgiven all your sins:

David also speaks of the blessing upon the man to whom God reckons righteousness apart from works: "Blessed are those whose lawless deeds have been forgiven, and whose sins have been covered. Blessed is the man whose sin the Lord will not take into account" (Romans 4:6-8).

God loved us even as sinners:

God demonstrates His own love toward us, in that while we were yet sinners, Christ died for us (Romans 5:8).

There is no condemnation to those in Christ:

There is therefore now no condemnation for those who are in Christ Jesus (Romans 8:1).

You are a temple of God:

Do you not know that you are a temple

of God, and that the Spirit of God dwells in you? (1 Corinthians 3:16).

You are sanctified in Christ:

Do you not know that the unrighteous shall not inherit the kingdom of God? Do not be deceived; neither fornicators, nor idolaters, nor adulterers, nor effeminate, nor homosexuals, nor thieves, nor the covetous, nor drunkards, nor revilers, nor swindlers, shall inherit the kingdom of God. And such were some of you; but you were washed, but you were sanctified, but you were justified in the name of the Lord Jesus Christ, and in the Spirit of our God (1 Corinthians 6:9-11).

The least honorable is most honored:

The members of the body which seem to be weaker are necessary; and those members of the body which we deem less honorable, on these we bestow more abundant honor, and our unseemly members come to have more abundant seemliness, whereas our seemly members have no need of it. But God has so composed the body, giving more abundant honor to that member which lacked, that there should be no division in the body, but that the members should have the same care for one another (1 Corinthians 12:22-25).

You are a new creature in Christ:

> If any man is in Christ, he is a new creature; the old things passed away; behold, new things have come. Now all these things are from God, who reconciled us to Himself through Christ, and gave us the ministry of reconciliation, namely, that God was in Christ reconciling the world to Himself, not counting their trespasses against them; and He has committed to us the word of reconciliation. Therefore, we are ambassadors for Christ, as though God were entreating through us; we beg you on behalf of Christ, be reconciled to God. He made Him who knew no sin to be sin on our behalf, that we might become the righteousness of God in Him (2 Corinthians 5:17-21).

You are holy and blameless:

> He chose us in Him before the foundation of the world, that we should be holy and blameless before Him (Ephesians 1:4).

We have boldness and confidence in Christ:

> This was in accordance with the eternal purpose which He carried out in Christ Jesus our Lord, in whom we have boldness and confident access through faith in Him (Ephesians 3:11,12).

We have redemption and forgiveness in Christ:

> . . . in whom we have redemption, the forgiveness of sins (Colossians 1:14).

We are blameless and beyond reproach:

> He has now reconciled you in His fleshly body through death, in order to present you before Him holy and blameless and beyond reproach (Colossians 1:22).

We are born again to a living hope:

> Blessed be the God and Father of our Lord Jesus Christ, who according to His great mercy has caused us to be born again to a living hope through the resurrection of Jesus Christ from the dead (1 Peter 1:3).

You are a chosen people:

> You are a chosen race, a royal priesthood, a holy nation, a people for God's own possession, that you may proclaim the excellencies of Him who has called you out of darkness into His marvelous light (1 Peter 2:9).

Your sins are forgiven:

> I am writing to you, little children, because your sins are forgiven you for His name's sake (1 John 2:12).

★   ★   ★

Many people have said, "I really try to be a good Christian but the harder I try the more I fail." But what does the Word of God say?

Live by faith:

> The righteousness of God is revealed from faith to faith; as it is written, "But the righteous man shall live by faith" (Romans 1:17).

We are freed from our old self:

> Our old self was crucified with Him, that our body of sin might be done away with, that we should no longer be slaves to sin; for he who has died is freed from sin. Now if we have died with Christ, we believe that we shall also live with Him, knowing that Christ, having been raised from the dead, is never to die again; death no longer is master over Him. For the death that He died, He died to sin, once for all; but the life that He lives, He lives to God. Even so consider yourselves to be dead to sin, but alive to God in Christ Jesus. Therefore do not let sin reign in your mortal body that you should obey its lusts, and do not go on presenting the members of your body to sin as instruments of unrighteousness; but present yourselves to God as those alive from the dead, and your members as instruments of righ-

teousness to God. For sin shall not be master over you, for you are not under law, but under grace (Romans 6:6-14).

God is our freedom:

I see a different law in the members of my body, waging war against the law of my mind, and making me a prisoner of the law of sin which is in my members. Wretched man that I am! Who will set me free from the body of this death? Thanks be to God through Jesus Christ our Lord! So then, on the one hand I myself with my mind am serving the law of God, but on the other, with my flesh the law of sin (Romans 7:23-25).

God's mercy does not depend on us:

It does not depend on the man who wills or the man who runs, but on God who has mercy (Romans 9:16).

God causes your growth:

Neither the one who plants nor the one who waters is anything, but God who causes the growth (1 Corinthians 3:7).

You are not your own; you belong to God:

Do you not know that your body is a temple of the Holy Spirit who is in you, whom you have from God, and that you are not your own? (1 Corinthians 6:19).

God comforts us:

Blessed be the God and Father of our Lord Jesus Christ, the Father of mercies and God of all comfort; who comforts us in all our affliction so that we may be able to comfort those who are in any affliction with the comfort with which we ourselves are comforted by God. For just as the sufferings of Christ are ours in abundance, so also our comfort is abundant through Christ (2 Corinthians 1:3-5).

Our adequacy is from God:

Such confidence we have through Christ toward God. Not that we are adequate in ourselves to consider anything as coming from ourselves, but our adequacy is from God, who also made us adequate as servants of a new covenant, not of the letter, but of the Spirit; for the letter kills, but the Spirit gives life (2 Corinthians 3:4-6).

God's glory is transforming:

The Lord is the Spirit; and where the Spirit of the Lord is, there is liberty. But we all, with unveiled face beholding as in a mirror the glory of the Lord, are being transformed into the same image from glory to glory, just as from the Lord, the Spirit (2 Corinthians 3:17,18).

Walk by the Spirit:

Walk by the Spirit, and you will not carry out the desire of the flesh (Galatians 5:16).

We are strengthened through God's power:

...that He would grant you according to the riches of His glory, to be strengthened with power through His Spirit in the inner man (Ephesians 3:16).

Put on the new self:

In reference to your former manner of life, you lay aside the old self, which is being corrupted in accordance with the lusts of deceit, and...be renewed in the spirit of your mind, and put on the new self, which in the likeness of God has been created in righteousness and holiness of the truth (Ephesians 4:22-24).

Think on worthwhile things:

Finally, brethren, whatever is true, whatever is honorable, whatever is right, whatever is pure, whatever is lovely, whatever is of good repute, if there is any excellence and if anything worthy of praise, let your mind dwell on these things. The things you have learned and received and heard and seen in me, practice these things; and the God of peace shall be with you (Philippians 4:8,9).

Set your mind on things above:

If then you have been raised up with Christ, keep seeking the things above, where Christ is, seated at the right hand of God. Set your mind on the things above, not on the things that are on earth. For you have died and your life is hidden with Christ in God (Colossians 3:1-3).

Become a cleansed vessel:

In a large house there are not only gold and silver vessels, but also vessels of wood and of earthenware, and some to honor and some to dishonor. Therefore, if a man cleanses himself from these things, he will be a vessel for honor, sanctified, useful to the Master, prepared for every good work (2 Timothy 2:20,21).

Christ cleanses us from dead works:

How much more will the blood of Christ, who through the eternal Spirit offered Himself without blemish to God, cleanse your conscience from dead works to serve the living God? (Hebrews 9:14).

God's grace cleanses us:

"Their sins and their lawless deeds I will remember no more." Now where there is forgiveness of these things, there is no longer any offering for sin. Since therefore, brethren, we have confidence to enter the holy place by the blood of Jesus, by a new and living way which He inaugurated for us through the veil, that is, His flesh, and since we have a great priest over the house of God, let us draw near with a sincere heart in full assurance of faith, having our hearts sprinkled clean from an evil conscience and our bodies washed with pure water (Hebrews 10:17-22).

Put away bad behavior:

Putting aside all malice and all guile and hypocrisy and envy and all slander, like newborn babes, long for the pure milk of the word, that by it you may grow in respect to salvation (1 Peter 2:1,2).

Become partakers of God's divine nature:

His divine power has granted to us everything pertaining to life and godliness, through the true knowledge of Him who called us by His own glory and excellence. For by these He has granted to us His precious and magnificent promises, in order that by them you might become partakers of the divine nature, having escaped the corruption that is in the world by lust. Now for this very reason also, applying all diligence, in your faith supply moral excellence, and in your moral excellence, knowledge, and in your knowledge, self-control, and in your self-control, perseverance, and in your perseverance, godliness, and in your godliness, brotherly kindness, and in your brotherly kindness, love. For if these qualities are yours and are increasing, they render you neither useless nor unfruitful in the true knowledge of our Lord Jesus Christ (2 Peter 1:3-8).

He is the propitiation (satisfaction) for our sins:

My little children, I am writing these things to you that you may not sin. And if anyone sins, we have an Advocate with the Father, Jesus Christ the righteous; and He Himself is the propitiation for our sins; and not for ours only, but also for those of the whole world (1 John 2:1,2).

We are purified:

Beloved, now we are children of God, and it has not appeared as yet what we shall be. We know that, when He appears, we shall be like Him, because

we shall see Him just as He is. And
everyone who has this hope fixed on
Him purifies himself, just as He is pure
(1 John 3:2,3).

★    ★    ★

Some people say, "I'll never make it." But
what does the Word of God say?

God is for us:

What then shall we say to these things?
If God is for us, who is against us?
(Romans 8:31).

Nothing can separate us from God:

I am convinced that neither death, nor
life, nor angels, nor principalities, nor
things present, nor things to come, nor
powers, nor height, nor depth, nor any
other created thing, shall be able to
separate us from the love of God,
which is in Christ Jesus our Lord
(Romans 8:38,39).

Be transformed by God:

I urge you therefore, brethren, by the
mercies of God, to present your bodies
a living and holy sacrifice, acceptable
to God, which is your spiritual service
of worship. And do not be conformed
to this world, but be transformed by
the renewing of your mind, that you
may prove what the will of God is,

that which is good and acceptable and perfect (Romans 12:1,2).

God is hope:

May the God of hope fill you with all joy and peace in believing, that you may abound in hope by the power of the Holy Spirit (Romans 15:13).

Put your faith in the power of God:

My message and my preaching were not in persuasive words of wisdom, but in demonstration of the Spirit and of power, that your faith should not rest on the wisdom of men, but on the power of God (1 Corinthians 2:4,5).

God provides a way to escape temptations:

No temptation has overtaken you but such as is common to man; and God is faithful, who will not allow you to be tempted beyond what you are able, but with temptation will provide the way of escape also, that you may be able to endure it (1 Corinthians 10:13).

Your toil is not in vain in the Lord:

Be steadfast, immovable, always abounding in the work of the Lord, knowing that your toil is not in vain in the Lord (1 Corinthians 15:58).

Our adequacy is from God:

Such confidence we have through Christ toward God. Not that we are adequate in ourselves to consider anything as coming from ourselves, but our adequacy is from God, who also made us adequate as servants of a new covenant, not of the letter, but of the Spirit; for the letter kills, but the Spirit gives life (2 Corinthians 3:4-6).

Our power is of God:

We have this treasure in earthen vessels, that the surpassing greatness of the power may be of God and not from ourelves (2 Corinthians 4:7).

Walk by faith, not sight:

We walk by faith, not by sight (2 Corinthians 5:7).

God's grace is sufficient:

He has said to me, "My grace is sufficient for you, for power is perfected in weakness." Most gladly, therefore, I will rather boast about my weaknesses, that the power of Christ may dwell in me (2 Corinthians 12:9).

Don't lose heart:

Let us not lose heart in doing good, for in due time we shall reap if we do not grow weary (Galatians 6:9).

Be strengthened with God's power:

> ...that He would grant you, according to the riches of His glory, to be strengthened with power through His Spirit in the inner man (Ephesians 3:16).

God is at work in you:

> It is God who is at work in you, both to will and to work for His good pleasure (Philippians 2:13).

I can do all things through Christ:

> I can do all things through Him who strengthens me (Philippians 4:13).

We are strengthened with all power:

> ...strengthened with all power, according to His glorious might, for the attaining of all steadfastness and patience (Colossians 1:11).

God has given us a spirit of power:

> God has not given us a spirit of timidity, but of power and love and discipline (2 Timothy 1:7).

Christ aids those who are tempted:

> He had to be made like His brethren in all things, that He might become a merciful and faithful high priest in things pertaining to God, to make propitiation for the sins of the people. For since He Himself was tempted in that

which He has suffered, He is able to
come to the aid of those who are
tempted (Hebrews 2:17,18).

God helps in time of need:

We do not have a high priest who cannot sympathize with our weaknesses,
but one who has been tempted in all
things as we are, yet without sin. Let
us therefore draw near with confidence
to the throne of grace, that we may
receive mercy and may find grace to
help in time of need (Hebrews 4:15,16).

We are equipped to succeed:

The God of peace, who brought up
from the dead the great Shepherd of the
sheep through the blood of the eternal
covenant, even Jesus our Lord, equip
you in every good thing to do His will,
working in us that which is pleasing in
His sight, through Jesus Christ, to
whom be the glory forever and ever
(Hebrews 13:20,21).

Job is an example for us:

Behold, we count those blessed who
endured. You have heard of the endurance of Job and have seen the out-
come of the Lord's dealings, that the
Lord is full of compassion and is mer-
ciful (James 5:11).

Divine power enables us:

His divine power has granted unto us everything pertaining to life and godliness, through the true knowledge of Him who called us by His own glory and excellence. For by these He has granted to us His precious and magnificent promises, in order that by them you might become partakers of the divine nature, having escaped the corruption that is in the world by lust. Now for this very reason also, applying all diligence, in your faith supply moral excellence, and in your moral excellence, knowledge, and in your knowledge, self-control, and in your self-control, perseverance, and in your perseverance, godliness, and in your godliness, brotherly kindness, and in your brotherly kindness, love. For if these qualities are yours and are increasing, they render you neither useless nor unfruitful in the true knowledge of our Lord Jesus Christ (2 Peter 1:3-8).

*Chapter Ten*

# Because God Loves Me

Many people have expressed how much the following paraphrase of 1 Corinthians 13:4-8 by Dr. Dick Dickinson has helped their self-image. Read it out loud every morning for a week or a month and see how your concept of God and His response to you will be changed.[1]

Because God loves me, He is slow to lose patience with me.

Because God loves me, He takes the circumstances of my life and uses them in a constructive way for my growth.

Because God loves me, He does not treat me as an object to be possessed and manipulated.

Because God loves me, He has no need to impress me with how great and powerful He is because *He is God,* nor does He belittle me as His child in order to show me how important He is.

Because God loves me, He is for me. He wants to see me mature and develop in His love.

Because God loves me, He does not send down His wrath on every little mistake I make, of which there are many.

Because God loves me, He does not keep score of all my sins and then beat me over the head with them whenever He gets the chance.

Because God loves me, He is deeply grieved when I do not walk in the ways that please Him because He sees this as evidence that I don't trust Him and love Him as I should.

Because God loves me, He rejoices when I experience His power and strength and stand up under the pressures of life for His name's sake.

Because God loves me, He keeps on working patiently with me even when I feel like giving up and can't see why He doesn't give up with me too.

Because God loves me, He keeps on trusting me at times when I don't even trust myself.

Because God loves me, He never says there is no hope for me; rather, He patiently works with me, loves me, and disciplines me in such a way that it is hard for me to understand the depth of His concern for me.

Because God loves me, He never forsakes me even though many of my friends might.

Because God loves me, He stands with me when I have reached the rock bottom of despair, when I see the real me and compare that with His righteousness, holiness, beauty, and love. It is at a moment like this that I can really believe that God loves me.

Yes, the greatest of all gifts is God's perfect love!

# *Footnotes*

## Chapter One

None

## Chapter Two

1. Guy Greenfield, *The Wounded Parent* (Grand Rapids: Baker, 1982), p.39.
2. Ibid., p. 99.

3. J.I. Packer, *Knowing God* (Downers Grove, IL: InterVarsity Press, 1973), p.37.

4. Maxwell Maltz, *Psycho-Cybernetics and Self-fulfillment* (New York: Grosset & Dunlap, 1970), pp.137-38.

# Chapter Three

1. Norman Vincent Peale, *Dynamic Imaging: The Powerful Way to Change Your Life* (Old Tappan, NJ: Fleming H. Revell, 1982), pp. 46-47.

2. Ibid., pp. 51-52.

3. Dale E. Galloway, *Dream A New Dream* (Wheaton: Tyndale, 1975).

4. Ibid.

5. Joseph Aldrich, *Self-Worth* (Portland: Multnomah Press, 1982), pp.2-3.

# Chapter Four

1. Walter Trobisch, *Love Yourself* (Downers Grove, IL: InterVarsity Press, 1976), p. 23.

2. Joshua Liebman, *Peace of Mind* (New York: Simon & Schuster, 1946), p. 71.

3. Snell and Gail Putney, *Normal Neurosis: The Adjusted American* (New York: Harper & Row, 1964), pp. 64-65.

4. Arthur DeJong, *Making It to Adulthood* (Philadelphia: Westminster Press, 1972), p. 129.

5. Lloyd Ahlem, *Do I Have To Be Me?* (Glendale: Regal Books, 1973), pp. 46-47.

6. Adapted from William Backus and Marie Chapian, *Telling Yourself the Truth* (Minneapolis: Bethany Fellowship, 1980), pp. 106-07.

# Chapter Five

1. W. Edgar Moore, *Creative and Critical Thinking* (Boston: Houghton Mifflin, 1967), pp. 295-96.

# Chapter Six

1. Maurice Wagner, *The Sensation of Being Somebody* (Grand Rapids: Zondervan Publishing House, 1975), p. 37.

2. Ahlem, *Do I Have To Be Me?* p. 71.

3. Ibid., p. 73.

4. Adapted from Norman Wright, *The Christian Use of Emotional Power* (Old Tappan, NJ: Fleming H. Revell, 1974).

5. Herman Gockel, *Answer to Anxiety* (St. Louis: Concordia, 1965), p. 156.

# Chapter Seven

1. Adapted from William Backus and Marie Chapian, *Telling Yourself the Truth* (Minneapolis: Bethany Fellowship, 1980), pp. 109-10.

2. Adapted from Dr. Jerry Schmidt, *Do You Hear What You're Thinking?* (Wheaton: Victor Books, 1982), pp. 32-33.

3. Ibid., pp. 192-94.

4. Adapted from John Lembo, *Help Yourself* (Niles, IL: Argus Publications, 1974).

5. Webb Garrison, "The Joy of Memorizing Scripture," in *Christianity Today*, Nov. 25, 1966.

# Chapter Eight

None

# Chapter Nine

None

# Chapter 10

None

# NOTES

# NOTES